Tallahassee Writers Association

SEVEN HILLS REVIEW
2018

Volume 23

The Seven Hills Review is an annual project of the Tallahassee Writers Association which highlights the winners of both the Seven Hills Literary Contest and the Penumbra Poetry Contest. All screening, judging, manuscript preparation, artwork, and other production tasks are volunteer efforts of the Tallahassee Writers Association and our contributors.

For the latest information on entering the 2019 Seven Hills Review, including categories and entry criteria, be sure to check for updates at **www.twaonline.org**.

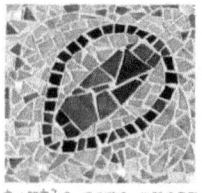

turtle cove press

Copyright © 2018 Tallahassee Writers Association

Published by Turtle Cove Press, Tallahassee, Florida

www.turtlecovepress.com

ISBN-13: 978-1-947536-01-2

Cover Photo: Bruce Ballister
Editors: M.R. Street and Bruce Ballister

Contents

*HM = Honorable Mention

The Judging Process

Our judges were selected for their expertise, experience, and standing in their specific category. Our readers are members of the Tallahassee Writers Association who donated countless volunteer hours reading through the often numerous submissions in their categories. All judging is blind; any entries with names attached to the primary submission were disqualified. These factors ensure that no preference is shown to submitters who may be known to our judges.

Each reader gave a yes, maybe, or no verdict on each submission. The results were made available to finalist judges through the Submittable software platform. Our finalist judges had the freedom to follow the recommendations of the pre-readers or to make their own determinations. In many of the categories, the judges agreed with our readers, but in a few, the search for the best required the additional effort.

We think you'll agree, some real gems have been found. Our winning writers span the globe with contestants from Portland, Oregon, to Salem, Virginia, to Surrey, England. This year we again had the result of authors winning in multiple categories.

Congratulations to all our winners.

To our readers, we hope you'll enjoy the 23rd volume of the *Seven Hills Review* and that you will follow up on the full versions of excerpted submissions. I welcome you to peruse the back of the book for brief biographies of our winners and judges. Thank you all.

Bruce Ballister, Contest Committee Chair
Immediate Past President
Tallahassee Writers Association

THE SEVEN HILLS LITERARY COMPETITION
2018

Creative Non-Fiction

Finalist Judge – Randi Atwood, Tallahassee, Florida

First Place

Trouble or Welcome to Milan

Peggy McCarthy – Columbia City, Indiana

"You going to be in trouble." Paola leaned long-legged and lean against the kitchen table while I dried dishes.

"Trouble?" I polished a plate.

"You going to get in trouble with men. I see it." She nodded and leaned back on her palms.

Hmm. I had trouble with men, all right.

The trouble was, they weren't interested. I didn't argue with my new employer, but I'd never even had a steady boyfriend. That had been embarrassing in high school--downright strange at age twenty-three.

I knew she was warning me, but if Paola thought I, of all people, might have man trouble, there might be just a glimmer of hope.

"Because...?" If she saw something the entire male population of Noble County, Indiana had missed, I wanted to hear it.

"You have a way," Paola said. "You look at men."

I set the last of the plates onto the stack and turned to her.

"You do. You look right at a man."

I snorted. "...And?"

"In America this is normal? You lookink at everyone you meet on the street?" She looked skeptical. "You look into a man's eyes? Say to him bon giorno?"

"Uhh..." I tried to take her seriously--dutifully remembered back.

It was my last trip into town. I was bubbling over. My bag was packed, my bank account cleared out, my car sold.

I'd passed a man—a stranger—on the street. I zeroed in on that sunny morning.

We had looked each other right in the eye. "Yes!" We both said good morning. "Yes," I said. "Everyone."

Absolutely.

"There." Paola spanked her hands together. "You see? You going to be trouble."

A howl rose from the back of the apartment. I stopped short.

Paola didn't even blink. "You going to be here for a year, you mus' learn about Italian men." I met her eyes and held up the little metal espresso maker I'd just polished dry. She pointed with her chin—of course; it hung on the wire rack over the sink. "You mus' give that thing a hard—is it 'scrub?' every time."

"Yes, scrub. I'll remember." The howl sharpened to a shriek. A door slammed. My heart jumped, but I took Paola's cue and reached into the sink for the last pot.

"If you don' clean it every time, the oils," she made a face. "They become very bitter. This," she waved a hand over her shoulder toward the ruckus. "Is not your problem." Paola shrugged. "On Monday, Fiona returns to England. Only then the crying becomes your problem, no?"

"You girls from the countryside." She shook her head. "You not accustomed to attencione. When a man works his charm, you believe. But you don' know Italian men." Paola puffed herself up, did a little table swagger. "They become hot, these men." Her softly spiked dark-red hair moved above her narrow shoulders. "They are proud to become animales in the summer."

I wrung out the dish cloth. There was more trouble down the hall.

Screams, pounding feet, slamming doors. Was someone being chased?

"Is nothing." Paola tapped a cigarette out of its packet and stood to pull a lighter from the pocket of her slacks. "Is bath time." She shrugged and pulled the corners of her mouth down.

Discipline was not my concern right now, but it would be. When Paola went out to the balcony to light up, I stepped into the hallway to listen at the bathroom door.

I was the wunderkind of children. My success was based on established codes of conduct and cooperation supported by the positive expectations of caring adults. Yes, exactly: in Sunday School terms. In clean, textbook language. I didn't know it yet, but my experience was naive in the face of this outrageous Italian family.

Paola had been very careful of my qualifications. Future Teachers of America and volunteering in Mrs. Buffembarger's second grade class had seemed important when I wrote them down. I was about to find out that Elementary Ed classes and teaching Sunday school didn't really apply.

"There's a good girl," Fiona muttered inside. "It's over now, silly thing. Quit your whining."

Five-year-old Elena was ejected like a white cocoon, still sniffling, into the hallway, her dark hair pixieish against the towel. Alessia and Stephano, eight and eleven, were sprawled in the hallway. They protected their crayons from Elena's scuffling feet with outstretched hands while Christina shrieked in the bathroom.

"Maggie, is so nice, the new colors!" Alessia twinkled up at me.

Christina yelled on the other side of the door. "You the only au pair who brings to us presents." She carefully filled pink into Cinderella's skirt. "This one, the hair is yellow, no?"

"That's right." The crayons lay like a bright picket fence, not scattered but lined up next to their boxes. "Why is Christina crying?"

And why doesn't it matter to anyone?

Alessia shrugged. "She's not like the bath. Elena!" She warned. "Don' touch the colors! You have yours!"

I eased Elena's foot away from the crayons. "Where are your pajamas?" She had recovered completely. Real tears sparkled on her lashes while she led me down the hall, but they only made her smile prettier.

In the bedroom she unself-consciously dropped the towel to step into short pjs. "What color are these?"

She slanted a look at me.

"I don't mean 'do you know what color.' I mean, 'what color in Italian.' In English, they're pink."

"In Italian, 'rosa.'" She smiled. "With fiori on it." Even with identical boy-cut hair and those deep brown eyes, the three girls were easy to tell apart. Elena's slenderness made her elfin.

"There's a good girl," Fiona sounded very British. And patient, muffled by the steamy air; determined. "Now to rinse." Christina's screams came in short gasps.

I opened the door. "May I?"

"Yes, certainly. Into the lion's den on your first day, then?" Fiona held Christina by the arm and forced her into a fluffy hooded terry-cloth robe. "I know it sounds frightful." She looked me in the eye. "This isn't even the worst of it." She pursed her lips and reached for a comb. "They were screaming when I arrived." Christina squirmed, but Fiona held her in a headlock and ran the comb across the top of her head. "They've never let up. There! It's over! Honestly, I should think a seven-year-old would be ashamed to behave so poorly. Now. Into your pajamas!"

~◇~

"Paola pretends she understands what this is like," Fiona and I swayed with the bus as it rounded a corner. "But, of course, when they lived in America they weren't servants. They weren't struggling to learn a foreign language."

I soaked in the sun on trees, the narrow street, Italians bustling into shops, snatches of overheard conversation.

"He taught at university, you see."

How did Fiona manage to look so very different from the Italians?

"They were honored guests in the States."

Her gray sweater, for one thing, screamed, "I'm not like you!" to the summer dresses and high-heeled sandals.

"Take note. This is the stop to catch the number one tram. *Paneteria Graciela* is just there, which offers, by the way," Fiona raised her eyebrows, "a lemon custard tart well worth the price."

The tram delivered us to the center of *Milano*. "They're cunning, the Cantabonis. They'll wring every last drop of work out of you." Fiona strode across the stone plaza on sensible shoes, a grey dove among small bright parakeets. "There's the American Consulate." Fiona gestured toward a huge columned building. "Mind, should you have trouble, you come here straightaway."

Would I remember where the Consulate was? And why did everyone think I'd have trouble? We plowed a serious line through children feeding pigeons on the wide stone steps, and detoured around tourists gathered around the men who manned carts of post cards and street food.

"Just here," she nodded," is the language school. You'll want to sign up for classes first thing, so Paola can't *forget*," she raised her eyebrows.

"Your mornings off." She glanced over her shoulder. "Come along—don't dilly-dally. These Italians," It wasn't just her British accent. Fiona pronounced *men* like a swear word. "Will pounce should they sense you're not exactly sure what you're about."

As if on cue, a man straight out of the movies with dark eyes and hair leaned toward Fiona. In passing, he blocked her path. "Ooh, get off, you!"

She swatted his arm with her furled umbrella—surely the only one out in public on a sunny day—and dodged.

"Ma, bel-la!"

He laughed and shrugged, looking back at her.

"You see? They're filthy! Don't look at him!"

I couldn't help it. He backed away as we left him behind, holding out his arms, smiling a protest. I smiled back and tilted my head.

"My god." Fiona looked horrified. "If he follows us, I swear I shall leave you to your own devices. Then see whether you find your way home."

It was true. I was at her mercy. What would I do without Fiona next week?

Well, one thing: I hadn't packed a gray wool skirt.

"Notice, Paola's had you take your Saturday off for June on the last day of May." We'd made the rounds of things Fiona said I should know—museums and the shopping galleria—while she pointed out bus and tram stops. Information started to run off my brain like rainwater off a slate roof.

On the tram heading home, my calves hummed with cramp. I eyed the flat hard bench seat, but Fiona stood, stolid and somber. "She's planned it all quite nicely, you see. This is my last day, who hasn't had a day off since April," Fiona slanted her eyes at me. "So it's the two of us off together, me escorting you round and you not due for another free day til July." She sniffed.

"Have you been here a whole year?" She didn't seem to like the kids at all.

"Me? Not bloody likely! The agency sent me just after Christmas." She gripped the overhead strap and leaned into the turn. "They had trouble with the last one." Fiona eyed me. "You won't stay either, most likely. Although it's different for you Yanks." She turned to look me up and down, considering how much to tell. "They do think they own you." She enunciated clearly. "You're a status symbol, you know. That little greeting committee wasn't friendliness. The whole building knew The Cantabonis' New American Au Pair," she raised her eyebrows. "Had arrived. They waited straight through *merenda* for you. Got quite restless they did, missing their lunch."

"Status symbol?"

"Oh, yes. You Yanks are known as hard-working. Industrious. Puritanical, really." She sniffed dismissively. "But, you see, we Brits can escape, can't we? We're just across the Channel." Fiona nodded toward Graciela's.

"There's your landmark, mind." She nudged me. "I suppose if you can't escape, there's nothing to do but buckle down and work through it."

Buckle down? Get through it?

Escape?

When Paola wrote with her decision—they'd narrowed down the applicants and she offered me the chance to live in Milan for a year--I sold my car, my record collection and phonograph, and scraped together the money for a one-way flight.

It was true, I didn't have much money. The ticket cost all of three months' rent plus the thirty dollars I got for my poor old Valiant. I'd left fifteen dollars in my savings account and folded four twenty-dollar bills twice into the lining of my red Samsonite.

"When they commence their little tricks it won't be a train ticket to London you need." Fiona narrowed her eyes at me. "And you haven't brought money for plane fare home, have you." It was confirmation, not a question.

I didn't need the fare home. I'd save my salary. I understood that fifty thousand lire—eighty-three dollars a month—wasn't up to 1975 pay standards. But as Paola had pointed out, my meals and room were provided.

What would I spend money on?

"I'm not going to leave." I looked out at the sun. I was in Milan!

"When my year's up I'll be ready to see Europe." I aimed to save six hundred dollars—a ticket home and twice that again for bed-and-breakfasts and a Euro-Rail pass--and I'd know the language. "This is the adventure of a lifetime."

"Yes, of course it is. And the Cantabonis know it."

"What 'little tricks?'"

She raised a finger to point out the stone wall that meant our stop was next. "Well, for one, they make sure you're good with the little darlings—you're not an axe murderer, you don't do pot—and then they make a few minor adjustments. They told you there's a maid? A cook?"

"Right."

"Well, the cook becomes ill. Oh, so unfortunate. But you'll do a few light meals, won't you, just until we find another? Don't look skeptical. It's a well-known dodge, and the Italians are the worst of the lot." We stepped down onto the sidewalk.

"And what will you do? Pack it in? Go weeping home to mum from your Adventure of a Lifetime?"

I was glad for the chance to observe before I dove headfirst into the deep end of the au pair pool. I was grateful for Fiona's advice—but I had to wonder how much she'd contributed to the disconnect and disorder.

That night I dreamed of sirens and huge angry insects. I woke on my narrow mattress to leg cramps and roaring traffic and a tangle of wails: all three girls at once. They were my responsibility the minute Fiona left--and she'd already packed her bags.

Fiona checked the fastenings on her carpetbag and left without saying good-bye. The kids showed no interest, so I was the only one to see her off.

As I pulled the door shut, I realized that the two of us were crossing that threshold in opposite directions. The household was no longer her concern.

"Mind you watch Stephano. He's a brute," she breathed when the two of us were alone in the elevator. "A right little Stalin." Fiona didn't quite look over her shoulder, but she had the furtive air of an escapee. "He's expected to be The Man of the House while his father is gone." She leaned forward and spoke quickly. "But he'll hurt one of them seriously one day."

The elevator door slid open. Fiona stepped out into the sun and took a deep breath.

A scream broke from above. Fiona glanced up toward the fifth floor, then met my eye one last time. "Mind—it's the United States Consulate." When she stepped around the corner, I was very alone. My connection to the English-speaking world had snapped. Now there was no outside observer to clarify, or to note what went on in the household. It was just them and me.

Second Place

The Mysterious Barricades

David Oates – Portland, Oregon

This was before she started being upstairs with sick headaches. Before sleeping in to nine o'clock, ten o'clock. Before the Valium, before the discovery of white wine. It was before I turned twelve, more or less. In those days I was used to her, of course. She kept a strictly clean and non-chaotic house, despite the three boys and the rooster husband. She deferred to him always, of course. But within her domain, we toed the line.

This is a person, I am trying to say, who awakened admiration. Whom I relied on, and hoped to please, for example by offering her little hand-sweaty bouquets picked on the long walk home from third grade, forth, fifth. And if I got up first in the morning, I might catch her sitting at the kitchen table, gazing out toward the LA basin perhaps not smogged up yet, with her big red-edged Bible flat on the yellow formica before her. No longer reading. Chin on hand. Motionless. If I walked down the carpeted hall quietly, I'd catch her like that. A kind of still life.

It made me wonder, *Is she sad?* She didn't look sad. She looked – something else.

That she coped at all is a wonder. Mom's family had been just herself, her mother, and her grandmother Nellie. That was it. What men she had known, they had disappeared. Her father, dead when she was six. Her little brother, taken in infancy. And Nellie's own absent-headed husband: there but not there, since the mysterious fall. A smiling vacancy. "Best jail I was ever in," was his all-purpose quip.

Our boy-clobbered house was often invaded by neighbor boys (Tommy and Scott), sometimes by the three cousins and their dad, our father's only sibling. Without warning we could get up a small male mob for water-balloons, horsing around, wrestling. Boy-smells, bathroom jokes, endless throwing-things, falling-out-of-things, silliness, dumbness. The works.

Hard to imagine what she made of the scene she found herself immersed in.

* * *

Mom and Dad came to hear me in my great hour. I was to read my fifth-grade essay at a school assembly, my first literary triumph (or nearly first: that I could recite two funny poems by Ogden Nash was already regarded as evidence of a significant future).

The topic was patriotic, something like "Why America Is the Best Country Ever." Maybe the prompt was more sophisticated but that's how we took it. And I went at that topic with an unnerving certainty. I had already heard plenty in my short life about the bad and pathetic Russians and, in contradistinction, the Greatness Of America, which had according to my essay a lot to do with being able to a) *have hot showers,* b) *drive in your own car,* and c) my big closer: *Go To the SUPERMARKET!!* This was about the time that giant-sized grocery stores had appeared with vast parking lots and the marvel of self-opening doors. The boys had to be prevented from spending the entire visit jumping on the rubber mat to trigger the hissing double glass panels. Inside, it was aisles and aisles of everything. It had a whole rack of comic books where we could lounge on the polished linoleum floor while Mom shopped. It is easy to imagine her relief.

I took my mother shopping again just a little while ago, before leaving for Paris. It offered a kind of bent nostalgia. Here I am, towering over her in my balding, stiltlike way, trying to help. She is still petite, still attractive – she has been a beautiful woman for how many decades now? – but in her nineties easily flustered. My help only makes her forget what she was thinking, what she came here for. I can see this. So. . . I claim to be interested in the magazine rack. "I'll just go read for a few minutes while you find what you need," is my line. I can see her relief, once again. In all these years she has never found a way to be comfortable under our gaze – ours and Dad's – our collective, judging, man-inflected way of looking at her. She couldn't hit, couldn't throw, and couldn't keep up with the banter. It left her flat and deflated. Weary, I think. (Yet with her girlfriends from church, how vivacious!)

In the school assembly, I shone brightly. She and Dad seemed to like me, they were proud. I was sure of it.

* * *

The essay contest must have been a by-product of that political year: Nixon versus Kennedy. At ten years old you just absorb what your parents believe. I heard them talking to the other grown-ups at the Baptist church. They all held that you couldn't elect a Catholic to the presidency, because he would just take orders from the Pope.

But when I watched the debate on television, Kennedy did not sound the way they said – like he was trying to fool us and turn the country over to that Pope (whoever he was). And then, at some point, I heard his speech about religion and politics. Probably just a little snip played on the news. It has become famous of course, so it is hard, at this point, to sift out what part I understood then.

What I remember is a vague discomfort. I had a feeling something was not right about this way of thinking. As if my parents were bending their view of things to get around something they wouldn't name. It was exactly the same feeling I had had when my other Grandma told me not ever to put pennies or nickels in my mouth. To clinch the point, she said, "A Negro might have touched them." She had a confident, erect way of holding her head, silver hair-do always exact. We were driving somewhere. I took the coins out of my mouth. But something was wrong with what she had said. It didn't make any sense. Who cared if someone touched something? It reminded me of the way our Grandpa talked about nuns when he saw them on the street – he had bad names for them. Otherwise, he was a very sweet old guy, whiskey-smell and all.

Adults had a way of talking that seemed to swerve invisibly, like something was in their way. But I didn't know what it was. Maybe they didn't either.

* * *

My dad and his brother had found land up in the pine-covered mountains south of Los Angeles, and they built roomy new twin cabins fifty yards apart for us to spend summers in. Better yet, Uncle Bob bought a fat, brown, black-maned Welsh pony, and stabled her right there. How lucky can a kid be? The cousin-boys named her Lassie. But of course we got to ride her, too, once we had learned how to handle the tack and all.

The mountain town was in a wide granite-rimmed bowl, blue-forested on its further edges in the summer haze. I knew how to walk out our back door and continue straight up the wooded slopes, making zigs and zags to lessen the steepness, but keeping on a general bearing to hit what we called the Long Trail. It went right along our side of the valley, climbing eventually toward a pass. I had walked on the Long Trail often enough. But on this day, I was trying it on top of Lassie. And I planned to go further than ever.

I had a peanut-butter sandwich in a brown paper bag folded under my belt on one side. I wore Penney's jeans cut off at the knee, and my own invention was to leave the severed pant-legs drooping around my ankles. I believed they were thus somewhat like boots, or boot-tops anyway. Such as one might wear while riding. I was already a lengthy child, loosely assembled, and my legs hung down around the pony's sides. We rode bare-back, with just a leather bridle and a simple bit. Of course Lassie outweighed any of us by a huge margin, and the bit did not really equalize the contest. She turned when we told her. Provided she felt like it.

Angling this way and that through the forest, we reached the Long Trail. I dismounted and we scrambled up onto its reassuring obviousness. I turned us left, toward the pass – toward what an older boy who lived there year-round had called "the Back Country." That sounded captivating. We would walk in that direction. I climbed back up, Lassie sighed, and on we rocked. In the solitude every turn and tree, every little view or sound seemed to be my own, like a quiet possession, a satisfaction.

About the time I was thinking of my peanut butter sandwich, the trail snaked up toward a sharp turn. At that point I could see a boulder, evidently dislodged from above right onto the path. Lassie trudged up and stopped about five feet short. Pitched one of her longsuffering sighs, her flanks expanding, then contracting dolefully. The trail went off to the right. The chunk of granite, thigh-high, just sat there in the turn. There was room to step around it.

I kicked with my tennis-shoe heels, twitched the reins. "Giddyup Lassie" I said in my bossy voice. Nothing. I repeated it; still nothing. I looked carefully: no snake. Nothing.

I got off to pull on the bridle-rope gently; then firmly; then at a near 45 degree angle, *insisting* that she follow me around the rock. But she had decided this was it, and now she just wanted to go home and see what might be in that manger.

I climbed back up on her sweaty back, unsure what to do next. The forest was quiet in its not-quiet way. The boulder, just there. And us. Just there in the pointed firs and long-needled pines and dusty trail-smell and clear sharp air.

Big black-speckled rock on the trail. It looked like the granite that poked up through the forest floor everywhere, sometimes big solitary boulders, truck-sized, house-sized, just sitting there in the forest, like they'd been dropped off. You could climb up to sit on one, twelve feet above anybody, and be like a little vizier, a quiet lord of the domain. It would have paintlike splotches, skintight, unpeelable: gray, and whitish, and bright yellow-green. Also mosses, dark and crispy in our dry summers. And a litter of cones and cone-bits shredded off by squirrels, plus twigs and whatnot you could flip down off the perch. And you would feel the unsmooth surface of the boulder marking your palms and your butt, like giant salt crystals. The shiny black bits we knew were called "mica" (confusingly like the book of the Bible), because someone had once showed us a wide smoky-transparent wafering of it in a hunk of split-open granite, like the inside of a piece of weird fruit. Mica.

I looked down at the obstructing rock, just a small cousin of the big boulders. I felt, if anything, friendly toward it.

But mostly I felt the forest itself, which often seemed almost to be sighing, a sound high up in the tall tops, that you might also feel passing on the soft of your cheek. It was just there, all around us. Like the beards of lime-green lichen dangling from limbs and trunks and creeping even out onto twigs and falling on the floor with the deadwood litter. It grew, it fell, it was just there. Where we were.

But what did it mean, after all? – Lassie, the refusal, the boulder and the quick turn and the long new trail, that stretched onwards to . . . well, it could be infinity for all I knew. I wasn't frightened, not by the what-was-lurking aspect. Though it was a little eerie. The silent moment.

There was no forest-fear. Forest was familiar to me, I played in it every day, it nodded in the windows of our sleeping-loft and (what we did not mention to the parents) we escaped down its branches sometimes, out the window on the back side away from the doors, to walk around and have night-adventures. Forest held snow in the winters, to sled under. And there were certain tall trees we climbed, to get to the very highest rungs where the trunk would, amazingly, have become slim enough to get your arms all the way around, to ride it back. . . and forth. . . across the shocking distance those treetops travelled even in a light breeze. They left pitch on your arms and your t-shirt and your jeans. That was all.

What I felt wasn't fear. It was a sense I had no words for. An odd calm. An unreadable presence.

After standing there in the not-silent silence for a while, Lassie sighed, turned around, and headed us for home.

* * *

A remembered evening, soon after, makes a strange twin to that moment in the forest – also silent, also overflowing. They are locked together in my mind.

Most summer nights we stayed outside playing after dinner all the way to nightfall, which came late. Mom had a piercing whistle, two fingers in the sides of the mouth like a cowboy or a coach, loud enough to summon us from blocks away. We were trained to come, *now*, when we heard it. Or else.

We had been playing hide and seek, all six of the brothers and cousin-boys. It felt exotic and wild to be playing so long and so late, there among the tall rough-barked trees, and we'd run like crazy after being discovered, flying for no reason in the dim light and the darkness and the warm air loaded up with vanilla-scent from the Ponderosa pines. She whistled and I came back to her first, by myself. I let myself in quietly, my head full of the fragrant dusk and the spin and hush of it all. And there in the big open room of the cabin she stood in semi-darkness, looking out the window. Her hair was reddish that summer but in the twilight just dark and full, banded across the top but falling free towards her shoulders. A rim of violet sky shone through the window from above the outline of dark pine-tops. There was a kind of glow coming in. And her motionless, staring out.

As if in amber, that moment. I don't mean love or sentiment or gratitude. Those are good things but they are not what I mean. It was the way my mother stood, silently, in that side-lighted gloaming. In her beauty.

What I mean is her *strangeness*.

Who was this person, after all? Like the forest. I felt them. I knew them, relied on them, trusted them. I loved them both, I knew that. In different ways. But they were so strange.

And what, after all, had they to do with me?

Third Place

Watermelon Kings

Tom Pelham – Tallahassee, Florida

Growing up on our family farm on Highway 79 in the rural Florida Panhandle in the 1950s, I learned to love watermelon at an early age. Every year when we planted a row or two of melons in the garden for our own enjoyment, I looked forward to the sweet taste of crispy red watermelon meat on a hot summer day. But that was before Daddy announced we were going into the melon business.

"I think we'll try a few acres of watermelons next year." That was Daddy's way of saying, "I am going to plant a lot of watermelons next year."

He made this announcement one winter evening in the mid-1950s as I sat around the supper table with my parents and three younger brothers. I was thirteen at the time. Because we depended on the farm to meet all of our family's needs, Daddy was always looking for ways to increase productivity so no one was surprised by what he said. But his announcement did set the rest of us to wondering what another crop would mean for our lives.

"What do we know about growing watermelons? We have never grown them before except for a few every year in the garden," Mama said.

"I've been talking to the farm extension agent. He says melons are easy compared to other crops, and he thinks our sandy soil will be ideal for them," Daddy said.

"How are we going to manage melons with all of the other crops we have to take care of?" I asked, thinking of the time we spent on cotton, peanuts, corn, hay, and the garden.

"Well that's the good thing," Daddy said. Watermelons are an early crop. We'll be finished with them in June before we start picking cotton in July."

Inwardly, I groaned, and in my mind the sweet taste of watermelon turned sour. It was clear that my younger brothers and I were going to spend even more time working in the fields.

Watermelons soon became one of our major crops. Early every spring, Daddy harrowed and fertilized the fields, throwing dirt into raised beds and leaving a drainage "dip" between the rows of melons. He showed us how to plant the seeds by hand using a hoe, making sure the plants would be about six feet apart in every direction to give the vines plenty of room to spread.

We quickly learned the varieties of melons: My favorite, the majestic Black Diamond, was shaped like a ridged, cylindrical pumpkin, its deep forest green skin so dark it looked black, with a golden underbelly, its ripened meat a rich royal red accentuated by shining black seeds concentrated around the edges of the rind. The exotic Congo, with its flamboyant coat of diffused silvery stripes running length-wise over its linear, medium green rind, had a pleasing taste but a more dispersed seed pattern. The elegant Charleston Grey, named for its solid light grayish color, was the seediest and sweetest of the three varieties. Because of its smooth skin and oval shape, the Grey was the easiest to handle and pack, and ultimately the melon of choice for Daddy. But we usually planted some of each variety.

Daddy liked to plant our melon crop early to beat other farmers to market while the prices were high. He especially worried about melons from down south. "If we lay around here on our lazy butts, those south Florida melons will flood the market and the bottom will fall out of the prices," Daddy said. "They won't taste as good as ours because they're not vine ripened, but the buyers won't know that."

So, he got more aggressive with the planting, starting earlier and earlier each year, with Mama warning him, "Roy, one of these years, we're going to get a late freeze, and it's going to wipe out the watermelon crop."

One day at school, the classroom door opened right after lunch. The principal stepped into the room and told the teacher I needed to come outside with him. Some of my classmates began to giggle, and I could feel my face blushing. "I bet he is going to get his butt whipped," I heard someone say, and I didn't doubt it because the principal loved to wield his big wooden paddle.

When I got outside, the principal said, "You need to come with me. Your father is waiting in my office." My anxiety level escalated into sheer terror. Daddy had never before come to the school house. Had the principal called him about something I had done? When we got to the principal's office, Daddy was there with my two younger brothers. "I hate to take them out of school, but I need them to help me this afternoon or I may lose my watermelon crop," Daddy said, and I began to breathe easier.

Although it was customary in our community for farmers to hold their children out of school to help harvest the crops, this was the first and only time Daddy and Mama pulled me or my brothers out to work. On the way home in our old Chevrolet pick-up truck, Daddy explained.

"The weather man is predicting a hard freeze with frost tonight, and I need ya'll to help me and your Mama cover up the young melon plants."

At home, Daddy got on the tractor, and Mama, my two younger brothers, and I piled into the trailer with a stack of old SearsRoebuck catalogs, and we headed to the melon patch. Daddy and Mama showed us how to place a sheet of paper from a catalog over the plants, and pile dirt on each end of the paper to hold it down. "Leave a little bit of open space to let the plants breathe," Daddy said. We all worked frantically to cover the biggest field of melons we ever had, finishing the last row well after dark by the light of the moon.

I do not know where Daddy got the idea to use the SearsRoebuck catalogs. Maybe it was born of pure panic. But it worked. The next day, after the frost disappeared and the cold front moved on through, Daddy walked the field inspecting selected plants, lifting their paper covers as gently as if he was handling a new-born calf. The plants survived except for a few killed by the frost because the wind blew off their covers. "We'll replant those and have a few late melons this year," Daddy said. We had averted the crisis.

Watermelon plants grow rapidly. Almost overnight, it seems, their long silvery green tendrils cover the beds, curling and intertwining with each other. Then come the colorful blooms that slowly wither away, leaving behind baby melons. After a plant had a half dozen or so melons the size of a pint mason fruit jar, Daddy showed us how to prune "the runts of the litter," the smallest ones and those damaged by the weather or varmints. "Pruning will help the good ones grow faster and bigger," he said.

Daddy watched over the melons like one of our mother hens minding her chicks. He seemed to know where each melon was located. "I noticed a couple of really nice Congos out by the fence this morning" or "I'll bet that Black Diamond by that old tree stump is going to top forty pounds before it's through growing," As he walked across the fields, he covered up melons with their vines to keep the sun from blistering them. When I heard, "God damned varmints," I knew he had found one pecked by the crows or ripped open by the swipe of a raccoon's claw. "I'll have to spread some poisoned grain for these thieving rascals." On a few occasions he hid in the bushes well before dawn, with his shot gun, hoping to kill one of the critters so he could hang it on a pole to scare the vandals away.

Harvesting melons involved heavy lifting that tested our endurance. But first we had to identify the ripe ones. Daddy taught us how to thump or slap a melon and judge its "ripeness" by the sound. "The hollower the sound, the riper the melon," he said. Using our pocket knives, we clipped the ripe melons at their stem and turned them "belly up" or stood them on end so we could identify them for pick up and hauling.

Next, Daddy, my brothers and I, and a couple of neighbor helpers formed a chain, handing or tossing twenty to thirty pound melons from one to another and placing them along the dirt "road" left open for our tractor and trailer. Then we lifted them up to be stacked in the trailer. The tractor driver hauled the melons to a large transport truck parked at the edge of the field in the shade of a giant live oak tree. Daddy hired the truck and its driver to haul the melons to market, usually Birmingham, Memphis, or Nashville.

Standing in the tractor trailer, one of us boys tossed the melons to someone in the transport truck who in turn handed them to the "professional" packer Daddy hired to help pack the melons. The packer placed each melon on top of two others laying side by side, and packed straw under, on top of, and between all of the melons to prevent shifting, bruising and "skinning" on the way to market. While I struggled to lift and toss the heavy melons, I watched the packer slip each one into its place, effortlessly it seemed to me, like a hand sliding into a familiar glove.

I recall one occasion when the melon truck arrived several hours late for our biggest harvest of the season, and we had to work into the night, our arms so heavy we could hardly lift them. With Mama driving the tractor, we loaded the trailer in the field by the tractor's head lights, and Daddy hung kerosene lanterns from tree limbs so that we could see how to load the truck.

Daddy was intent on leaving for Nashville that night, so we did not break for supper. Instead, he cut open a couple of watermelons, but I did not eat any that night or during the rest of the melon season. I had lost my taste for watermelon.

When we finished loading the truck about nine o'clock that evening, Daddy rushed home for a quick bath and change of clothes before he and the driver took off on the seven or eight hour trip to Nashville.

"Roy, why don't you get some sleep and leave in the morning?" Mama asked. "You're tired, and it's dangerous to be driving at night on strange roads with no sleep. You know what happened to Chance Roberts." Mr. Roberts, a local farmer, had died when his truck loaded with melons crashed and burned on a steep hill outside Birmingham.

But Daddy was undeterred. "I want to get the melons to Nashville by the time the market opens in the morning." A day or two later, he returned safely, tired from the long drive and sleeping on the straw in the back of the truck, but satisfied with the hard-earned money in his pocket.

After the last big harvest each season, Daddy scoured the field for any remaining melons that might be marketable. "Every good melon is at least a quarter or fifty cents or maybe even a dollar," he said. "And that beats feeding them to the hogs." So, on a Friday or Saturday afternoon, he took a pickup full of the last melons to town, hoping to sell them to grocery stores.

He usually returned with an empty truck because he always sold the melons at some price, even if he had to park on the street and sell them to passersby.

To sell the remaining good melons, Daddy turned my brothers and me into entrepreneurs. On Saturdays, he set up a bare bones roadside stand consisting of a pile of melons under a large live oak tree next to Highway 79, two old metal frame folding chairs, and a crude handmade road sign, "Vine Ripe Watermelons, $1 a melon, or 3 for $2."

"Daddy, nobody is going to stop and buy these old melons," I said.

"You just wait and see. When these big shots in their fancy cars come driving down out of Alabama on their way to Panama City Beach, they are going to see you tow-headed boys, and they are going to want to buy some melons. I bet they will even give you a tip." Daddy threw back his head and laughed. "Just you wait and see."

My brothers and I settled down in the old chairs, tired of working with watermelons and thinking we were wasting our time. But before long, a car slowed and pulled off the road. A middle-aged man got out, walked over to the pile of melons, and slapped a couple of them. "Boys, are these melons any good?" he asked.

"Yes sir, they are vine-ripe, real sweet. We grew them here on our farm," I said, surprised to hear Daddy's words coming out of my mouth.

"Is that right," he said, laughing. "Then I guess I will take three. Here is a five dollar bill. You boys are working hard so you can keep the change."

My mouth fell open in surprise. "Yes sir, thank you. Let me put them in your trunk for you."

We watched the highway with new enthusiasm. When we saw a vehicle coming, we waved at the approaching drivers with one hand and pointed at the melons with the other. By the end of the day, we had sold most of the melons and collected quite a few tips. Even Daddy was surprised when we told him how well we had done. We felt like watermelon kings when he told us we could divide the tips among us. Maybe the watermelon business isn't so bad after all, I thought.

When Daddy was convinced that no marketable melons remained in the field, it was clean-up time. He had us go through the field and load the trailer with deformed and defective melons that were not fit for people to eat. We hauled them to the hog pens and watched the swine go crazy as we tossed the damaged melons to them. Daddy's philosophy in the fields was the same as it was at the dinner table. "Clean your plates, boys. We don't want to waste anything."

Flash Fiction

Finalist Judge – Anna Yeatts, Pinehurst, North Carolina

First Place

Cease Fire

John Koelsch – Salem, VA

1968. Vietnam – The Michelin Plantation. On point for a battalion force of over five hundred men, we move through the rubber trees which provide shade from the sun but no surcease from the heat. My nerves are raw because of the Colonel's emphatic command.

"Anyone in the trees is fair game. Shoot first, shoot second, shoot last. I want bodies."

We are remiss in following said order. Two guys dressed like C.I.A. clerks in short sleeve white shirts with narrow black ties drive an American Jeep through the trees. Partly surprise and partly because no apparent threat exists, we call "Laddymau" and they come in.

Through our interpreter they claim to be just guys visiting their families.

Good excuse.

I think.

Not necessarily true, but good. I'd stick with it.

The Colonel is pissed they aren't dead. No evidence they are or aren't the enemy. The Colonel, his temples throbbing, reiterates his order, "Kill on sight! Period. Just kill!"

No problem with killing. Without cause is a concern. It's hot. I'm sweaty and tired. I don't much care. We move on.

We pass a village located outside the trees. In a hundred meters we'll change course and head deeper into the woods. We almost make it. Then the most inappropriate, horrific, terrifying apparition that can be imagined chugs its way into the woods. A freakin' yellow school bus!

I react at hypersonic speed yelling, "Hold your fire!"

I respond a tiny bit faster than that and fire a warning shot.

My men react on cue. Hundreds of rounds ventilate the bus and everyone on it. The bus driver bounces like a jack-in-the-box as sixty rounds riddle him. A young girl, maybe twelve, jumps from the back of the bus, her right arm twisted at a strange angle, blood all over her side. A woman has half her head blown off. Other people die and more are injured in the ensuing mayhem.

I scream, "Cease Fire! Cease Fire!"

The shooting continues. Combat veterans, once firing, are always loathe to cease. The world thunders. The bus smolders.

"Cease Fire!" The shooting stops.

"Cease Fire!" Rings silently through the trees. The words burn forever.

Someone gets the bus into reverse. The gears grind and it backs slowly into the village.

I stare into darkness, 'Cease Fire!' lashes my ears.

The Colonel runs up to me and shouts, "You didn't shoot those people, did you?"

That was the last round I ever fired in service of my country.

CALL OF DUTY

She won't believe I'm not the same person. Four combat tours in ten years—insanity is the best to be hoped for. Or maybe, just not surviving. But to not change? That ain't reality.

I joined. Thought I should serve my country. Beat opportunities in food service. Didn't consider consequences or what duty might require. Combat was exciting ... at first. Challenging.

That didn't last, but I was proud of doing my job that first tour.

The second tour ... brutal ... too much blood ... too many dead. I still did my job, but with less pride and more hatred. I killed those suckers. They deserved it. I hurt. Hurt bad inside.

Really thought I'd done enough.

Couldn't give it up though. Pulled a third tour "for the guys." They needed me. I thought I could keep them alive. At least ... some of them. Sometimes there was nothing I could do.

Nothing ... that's what I felt ... nothing. Still standing— pretty much dead.

I should have ended there.

Didn't.

Then the Army sucked me in with the same argument I used to sell myself on the third tour. "You're experienced, you're a top-of-the-line leader, you're needed to keep good men alive." All true. All BS. All of little concern because there wasn't much me left.

Now I'm divorced. Unable to sleep. Can't connect with anybody. Afraid to return to my old job as a police officer. On the street, I would explode and somebody would die.

A patriot—

A combat leader—

A disciplined warrior—

A veteran—

I answered the call of duty. I did my job, long past caring. Now, I have the rest of my life to count the cost.

No. I'm not the same person at all.

WE DID THE JOB

A rational explanation, that's all I want. Is that too much to ask?

Of course, most wars don't come with rational explanations. They come with a call to service.

I answered that call. Reluctantly, to be honest. I signed up for a non-combat job. Two years later, after I made a series of small, seemingly inconsequential decisions, I found myself assigned as a combat platoon leader in a shooting war in Vietnam, Republic of.

No explanation, rational or otherwise.

Just a job to do.

My choice—first, accomplish the mission; second, keep my men alive to go home. All else—chaff.

We did the job.

Two and a half million served in Vietnam. An estimated million, six-hundred thousand in combat, with over three-hundred thousand purple hearts awarded. Fifty-eight thousand two hundred and seventy-two names are etched in black granite—the heroes.

No explanation.

We did the job.

Under fire, George carried a wounded buddy to safety; Tiger One rained down destruction on Charlie from his Huey Cobra; Doc, routinely, pulled guys back from the brink to life; Keith died with six others when his chopper was shot down flying where it didn't belong, trying to help out.

Explanations?

Reasons?

We did the job.

Some of the place names are famous—Ashau, Cu Chi, Hamburger Hill, Hue, Khe Sanh, the Mekong Delta,—my own playground the Michelin—the Parrot's Beak. Others—spots in the jungle, trails in the mountains, rice paddy after rice paddy, streams in the Delta—no names, just places where we fought, killed ... died.

Never sure why, but ...

We did the job.

We returned to a Country in deep turmoil; at war with itself over what was just and what was wrong. A lot like it is today. We got caught in the crossfire. Lots of reasons proffered, justifications offered. No sale then or now.

I have found no explanations, but this I know:

Our country called.

We answered.

We did the job.

Second Place

Branded

Thomas Pelham – Tallahassee, Florida

One fall afternoon after school, I watched Daddy branding new calves. He heated the branding iron in an open fire and then stamped the calves on their rear flanks while they stood in the branding pen. The calves bleated loudly as they were branded. "Doesn't that hurt them," I asked. "Only for a minute," Daddy said, "and they heal quickly."

The next morning, before I caught the school bus, my brother Richard, who was only three years old at the time, was playing with me on the floor in front of the fire place. The fire place was spitting and crackling as the flames attacked the wooden logs. Mama had stepped outside for a few minutes to get something from the smoke house. She had warned me to stay away from the fire and to watch out for Richard.

As Richard and I played in front of the fire place, I said, "You are just a little calf, and I am going to brand you." I picked up an empty coca cola bottle from the floor, held the top in the fire for just a moment, and stamped him on his forearm, never thinking that the bottle was hot enough to burn him. Richard immediately cried out and continued to whimper as he rubbed his arm. "It will only hurt for a minute," I said, trying to comfort him while watching with alarm as an angry red ring formed on his arm. "It will heal quickly so don't tell Mama about it."

All day at school, I worried about what I had done to Richard and dreaded what might be waiting for me when I got home. My worst fears were realized when Mama met me at the front door.

"Did you burn him?" she demanded, pointing to the small red circle on Richard's arm.

"Yes, Ma'am, but I didn't mean to. I was just playing like I was branding him."

"Well, go and get me a peach tree switch because I am going to brand you."

And she did.

Third Place

Barracuda

Sydney Watson – Eastpoint, Florida

I was eating a grouper sandwich and having a cold beer. Black Beard's had the freshest fish on Grand Bahama.

I'd had a long day working the backwaters as a bonefish guide. My wife had been off the island for over six months. She'd had enough of my womanizing...that, and her career going south. I'd had plenty of time to think about what would happen to me if she left me for good. I'd made up my mind and my sometimes-too-selfish heart to get her back.

The bleached blonde who entered, accompanied by friends, was tall and thin. Her angular face accentuated her mouth, teeth too large. Not my type.

"Do you care if I sit?" she asked, crowding me and my grouper.

"No," I lied.

"Married?" she asked as she glanced at the band I never took off, not even in the tough times.

"Married. Wife off the island." I didn't want to engage in small talk and took another bite of my fish.

"Not married. No kids. I'm a direct woman, and I couldn't care less about the wife. By the way, my name's Lee," she offered. As we made eye contact, something seemed oddly familiar about her.

She had taken me by surprise. No games. Interesting.

"Tom," I replied, briefly touching her hand. "Can I buy you a drink?"

"Sure," she smiled, exposing her expensive dental work. This one didn't need a fisher boy, I mused.

"Actually, why don't you finish your food, and we can have that drink at my place?" She focused her attention on me. Strangely, all I could envision was a hook caught in that big mouth of hers.

We left, and I followed her expensive Lincoln in my rusted Jeep to Reef Drive, a neighborhood of million-dollar houses.

We never got to the drink. The house tour ended in the bedroom. Usually, I'm a first responder. Tonight was different. She took control. Like I said, I'd been thinking about the wife...

As I looked closely at her afterwards, recognition dawned on me. Scandal had rocked the island. My wife had been the journalist who'd covered the case, subsequently losing her job. The headline: *Ex-Pat Shot by Wife.* Eventually, she'd bought her way out. Murder had been dubbed suicide.

"You're Ted Pritchard's widow, or is it murderess?" I asked, repulsed at the sight of her.

Her mouth, carnivorous teeth gleaming, looked predatory. "You and your silly wife. Now your destruction is complete. You slept with the woman she couldn't put behind bars," she spat.

What do you do to kill a very large barracuda with sharp teeth? You gaff 'em. Taking her by surprise, I leaned over, grabbing the metal lamp, the next best thing, sinking the triangular tip through her neck.

She fell back, surprise and shock, mingling with fear.

"You know," I said with revulsion, "barracuda aren't even fit to eat. That makes you worthless."

I got out of bed and left, never thinking I'd kill a 'cuda that night.

Children's Chapter Books

Finalist Judge – Carol "Boots" Hensel, Panama City, Florida

First Place

Manny's Mural

Carol Bullman – Dallas, Texas

When Manny got home from school, he found his mother standing on a big sheet of plastic in his room. White paint trickled down her right arm.

"This wall was looking shabby," she said. "I thought your room could use a little sprucing up."

"I wanna help!" Manny said.

"Change into your grubbies, and you can give it a try." His mom trotted downstairs.

Decked out in his oldest jeans and a tee shirt that was a bit too snug, Manny dipped the roller into the milky paint and pressed it to the wall. Paint oozed down.

As if the roller were a prism, the paint spread into a rainbow of colors. Each line of dripping paint had within it a multitude of hues, so that one dribble might be pink on top, then magenta, purple, blue, then turquoise, and green.

Manny dropped the roller.

Pure white splashed onto the drop cloth.

He peered into the paint can . . . just plain paint.

Picking up the roller again, he made big strokes on the wall, up and down. His heartbeat sped and his eyes opened wide as he took in the miracle. Vigorously he worked until the paint on the roller grew sparse, and he had to stop and reload it. He stepped back. A detailed mural was appearing on his bedroom wall. It reminded him of the picture of the Sistine Chapel ceiling his father had shown him.

"Mom!" Manny called. "Come look!"

Manny heard his mother's footsteps racing up the stairs.

"Avemaría," she gasped.

Manny watched her eyes trace the wall in awe before coming to rest on the soggy white roller he was clutching. "I don't understand," she said.

"Me neither, Mom," Manny said as he spread some more paint on the wall and new portions of the picture emerged.

"May I try?" Mom asked, grabbing the roller. But, in her grasp, the paint remained white—large streaks of winter through the colors of spring.

When Manny took the roller back, he traced over the lines his mother had made, and the snow melted into explosions of blooms.

"Manny," his mother whispered, "you have been given a mysterious gift." She sat in silence, then, watching him. For an hour, Manny was mesmerized by the flashes of colors unfolding before him. He rolled on the paint in huge swipes, uncovering more and more of the beautiful scene.

Soon, Manny became accustomed to the wonders he was creating. "My arm is getting tired," he said.

"Let me bring you a snack," his Mom offered. "You just need a short break." After Manny ate the peanut butter crackers and apple slices, he felt like relaxing in front of the television.

"But Manny," his mother urged, "don't you want to finish the mural? Don't you wonder what will appear next?"

"I'll paint later, Mom," Manny said as he flopped down on the couch. When he had finished watching cartoons, he played a video game.

Just as the desire to get back to painting bubbled within him, Manny's dad got home from work. He was grumpy because he'd skipped lunch to attend a meeting.

"Dad, there's something amazing I have to show you!" Manny said.

"After dinner!" Dad said. "I can't do or say another thing until I've eaten."

Mom scrambled a few eggs and Manny put a stack of tortillas in the warmer to bake.

Finally, dinner was eaten. Dad's smile returned, and Mom excused Manny from dishwashing duty. "Go show your father the miracle," she said, shooing them upstairs.

Dad looked at the vibrant wall and the can of ordinary white paint. His mouth fell open.

After a moment, he said, "Is this some kind of trick? The wall was pale blue just this morning."

"I'll show you," Manny said. He picked up the roller and loaded it with paint. Then he proudly started smoothing paint on the wall.

A lump formed in Manny's throat. Thick, white columns rose up beside the lush colors.

"But the wall isn't finished!" Manny cried.

Mother came puffing into the room. "What's wrong?"

"My gift is gone!" Manny said.

Mother put her finger to her lips and thought for a moment. "Or perhaps," she said, "it's just resting." She patted his back, and his father tousled his hair.

The next day, when no one was looking, Mannytried to paint again. White. He tried the next day and the next. White. Plain white. The magic had vanished just as mysteriously as it had arrived.

Manny moped around the house. He didn't feel like watching TV or playing video games. He didn't want to do anything if he couldn't paint. He missed the feeling of the roller in his hand—he missed being a creator of beauty.

Each night, after his parents tucked him into bed, Manny would turn on his lamp and stare at the unfinished mural until tears blurred his view. One night, his dad came back, bringing Manny a bedtime snack of toast and milk.

"Son," Dad said. "You can finish that mural."

"But I don't know how to paint," Manny whispered, looking away.

"You can learn," Dad said.

Hues of hope swirled through Manny's imagination.. . .

Early the next morning, Manny found a brand new set of paints and brushes outside his bedroom door. The magic returned. But, this time, it wasn't the kind of magic that surprises people or even the kind of magic that can be seen. It was the kind of magic that echoes something already known.

Manny felt it flutter in his stomach. . .

Through years of practice, Manny learned to create beauty with a brush. He painted exquisite murals at schools and at nursing homes. When people patted his arm and said, "You have brightened our world," Manny smiled and raised his brush to a new section of wall. With each stroke, he became more of who he already knew he was.

Second Place

A Golden Fairy Story

Katie Clark – Tallahassee, Florida

Elif yawned and stared out the window. Mourning doves flittered and tweeted their song; she followed their rainbow wings until they flew out of sight.

"Elif, do you know the seven sacred colors of our people?" Ms. Sleigh asked.

"Gold, bronze, turquoise, emerald, ruby, amethyst, iridescent," she replied. At least the teacher asked an easy question.

"Does anyone know why these are our sacred colors?" Ms. Sleigh looked upon the class of thirteen legna students in various states of daydream. "Anyone?" The students seemed to all have discovered that their desks were intensely interesting. One student even had conveniently dropped his pencil on the earthen floor and had crawled under to retrieve it.

Sighing, Ms. Sleigh continued, "Very well. These are the colors that you will all become one day. If you are lucky, you will be an amethyst."

Elif thought about this and frowned. Her dreams of late had consisted of forever being the same color, never amounting to anything great.

Ezmerelda, sitting in the front row, asked, "Is it true that once your wings develop, your skin changes from gold to bronze?"

Merle chimed in, "Yes! My sister's wings just finished filling in. She is two years older."

Ms. Sleigh pulled at her pointed ruby ear, excited to finally see interest in her lesson. "Does anyone else have a color story they want to share?"

"My brother just cast his first spell last full moon, and he is now turquoise," Drew stated.

Elif tried to imagine her sun kissed skin changing to a different color, but just couldn't. She sighed and slumped down in her desk.

Walking down the aisle to Elif's seat, Ms. Sleigh asked, "Elif, "Do you have any questions?"

Her amethyst flecked eyes stared patiently at the downcast fae.

"Well, it is just that...I mean...what would happen if you never grew any wings and you stayed gold all your life????" Elif gestured wildly with her hands and returned the teacher's intense gaze.

Smiling, Ms. Sleigh replied, "Elif, you feel the same as many other young legna have felt at your age. You long to start the changing process, but don't try to do it too soon! Trust me, everyone will change, at their own pace, but everyone will change."

Elif considered her words, and hoped for them to be true. Her dreams just held her in their sway just so...

Ms. Sleigh returned to the front of the room to flip the lecture poster. As she passed the first row, Elif heard a whisper from Merle to Drew.

"Not every Fae changes. The snogard never change; my brother said so." Drew looked around as if this information was something he shouldn't know.

Snogard?

Elif pondered, but Drew offered no other information and returned his attention to Ms. Sleigh. Elif tried to follow the history lesson, but after a while she turned her gaze out the window and wondered when this tiresome class would be over. The ant that she caught on her way from singing lessons needed food and a companion.

"Psst." Elif jumped to see Drew sitting next to her. "Drew..." Elif whispered back.

"What are you looking at out there?" he asked.

"See that bee?" Elif pointed to a purple and green striped insect zipping by the window. "Yeah, it is just a bee," Drew replied.

"I am wondering where it goes after it visits these flowers."

"Back to its hive, I guess." Drew pushed back his long, golden hair behinds his pointed ears. "I never much thought of it. Why don't you ask Mr. Eevy? I am sure he would know."

"I know he would, but I don't want to be a pest. He seems to have more important things to do than to answer a little legna's questions all day. The last time I asked him about the spider I found, he ended up shooing me away and asked why I wasn't shaping flowers like most of the other girls...." Elif looked down at her desk and sighed.

"Oh, don't listen to him, Elif. Flowers make your room smell nice and all, but it is so much cooler to watch a spider spin its web."

Drew picked up Elif's twig pencil and began to doodle spider webs on her blank paper. He ended the spider webs a quarter of the way across the paper, and doodled a girl fae picking flowers along the bottom. He put down the pencil and began to hum quietly. As he hummed, the doodle spider dropped from the web onto the flower girl, and the flower girl dropped the flowers and ran off the side of the paper.

Elif giggled. "How did you do that?"

Before Drew could explain, Mrs. Sleigh asked, "Drew, Elif, did you two hear what I said about the 100-year emerald war?"

Elif and Drew replied, "No." Drew quickly crumpled up the paper and attempted to hide it in his sleeve.

"I see," Ms. Sleigh said. "Drew, I will take that." She held out her slender hand and waited expectantly.

Drew said, "But.. It's nothing." Giving Elif a fearful glance, he folded his arms and refused the teacher's request.

"If it's really nothing, then you wouldn't mind me looking at it. Give it up or face the consequences," she demanded.

At this point all the other students had ceased pretending to be completing their work; all eyes were peeled onto the pair, awaiting Drew's decision.

Elif shrugged her shoulders and nodded her head. There was no use arguing over a silly piece of paper. Sighing, Drew unfolded his arms, reached inside his sleeve, and handed over the paper in question.

Furrowing her eyebrows in dismay, Ms. Sleigh said, "Because you two are more intent on idle doodles, you can join me for a review session after the dinner hour."

"But, Ms. Sleigh," started Elif, "I have important work that needs to be completed!" She again thought back to the ant hidden in her desk.

"You should have thought of that earlier and paid more attention to the lesson," Ms. Sleigh replied. "You can finish it after you make up my work."

Turning to the class, she continued, "As for everyone else, do not forget to complete your essay on the importance of our colors in the 100-year emerald war. Class dismissed." She walked back to the front of the room, placed the paper on her desk and flipped the lecture chart back to the first page.

Elif stuffed her belongings into her leaf-woven satchel and stomped out of the classroom.

The clear, bright green skies that greeted her departure did nothing to improve her mood.

"Hey, wait up!," Drew struggled to catch up as he lugged his satchel and instrument case over his shoulders.

Elif stopped and kicked the blue grass in aggravation. "It's not fair! We didn't do anything wrong. It's not as if she was going over anything important."

"Don't let it get to you. It's not as if she could get you expelled for it. Let's just go to dinner and forget about if for an hour. Besides, I can get us seconds on dessert." He raised his golden eyebrows waiting for her reply.

She looked around at the classrooms of White Willow School neatly tucked inside the roots of the elm trees. Cerulean leaves rustled in the wind, adding their hue and song to the bustle of the multi colored Legna headed to the dining hall.

Shaking her head, she replied, "You go. I have TWO review sessions to attend now. In music class, Mr. Percy just didn't comprehend that I can't play the lute OR read the music, no matter how hard I tried. I really have something important that I need to do."

"Ok, but I'll save you a dessert anyway," he said and joined the throng of fairies headed to the dining hall.

"Thanks!" she shouted. "Just don't get caught!"

She watched him wave his hand and continue to dinner. After looking around and making sure that no teachers were watching, she turned the other direction and sprinted past the girls dorms and into the brush behind.

Reaching inside her satchel, she pulled out a clear container, gently sat it on its side, and opened the top. A purple ant the size of her hand inched its way out.

"I was going to keep you, but I just won't be able to," she said.

The ant crawled a short distance and then turned back towards her. "Thank you for setting me free, little one."

Startled, Elif replied, "I didn't know that ants could talk."

Nodding his little head, the ant said, "Yes, silly Legna, don't you know that all creatures can talk? You just have to listen."

"Ok, I will remember that. Thank you. My name is Elif."

"Trouble is my name; and I already know yours. Everyone knows yours." Without any further explanation, he retreated into the dark blue brush, leaving Elif to ponder his words.

Third Place
Daniel & Elizabeth and the Wild Kitty
Lyla Ellzey – Tallahassee, Florida

"What is it now, Daniel?" Elizabeth heaved a huge sigh. She was dressing her newest Barbie doll in a brand new outfit she and Mom had bought at the mall when Daniel called to her.

She didn't have time for another of Daniel's wild goose chases. She'd rather he leave her alone.

"No, seriously, Elizabeth. Look at this," Daniel insisted. "He's just the cutest thing you've ever seen."

"Okay. If I have to." Elizabeth laid her Black Dress Barbie among the various black dresses mom had let her get to go with the original short dress that Barbie was wearing. She'd planned to dress her in the long black evening gown next. Then she would dress Ken, Barbie's boyfriend, in his tuxedo and the two would have a lovely date riding in his red sports car. They'd probably go out to a fancy ball where they would dance for hours.

"Come on, Elizabeth!" Daniel urged. "If you don't hurry up, the cat will be gone."

"All right! I'm coming, Daniel." Elizabeth rose from her position where she sat cross-legged on the porch floor. She and Daniel called it sitting "Indian-style." They'd seen a western movie with Mom where all the Indian braves sat cross-legged around their campfire. When they needed to get up, they simply rose straight up without moving their feet.

She and Daniel had practiced for days, it seemed, before she could do it without wobbling all over the place. It took another day for Daniel to rise from his seated position. Every time he had tried to do it, he tumbled over sideways, or fell down halfway up. But, as he pointed out, he was two years younger than she. Of course, since she was older, he'd said, it was easier for her. Hah, she thought. It was still really hard to do. But, she couldn't let her little brother beat her, so she'd worked at it, carefully concentrating on standing up. And she did! Daniel didn't even congratulate her. He was so jealous that she did it first. Little brothers! They're always a bother. But, she had to admit he was a pretty neat kid. Sometimes. She loved being ten, and that was two whole years older than Daniel. He was just eight.

"There he is." Daniel pointed way to the back of their big yard as Elizabeth joined him on the patio.

"Where?"

"Look, Elizabeth. There. By the cedar tree we planted last year. See, he's moving."

Daniel let out a squeal. "He's going to run away. Don't let him get away, Elizabeth!"

"But, I don't see him," Elizabeth wailed.

"He's right there!" Daniel started across the back yard toward the cedar tree. It was then that Elizabeth saw a little scraggly tan cat of some kind. The bottom of the tree came all the way to the ground and the little cat was hiding among its bottom branches.

"Oh," Elizabeth said, stopping in her tracks. "Stop, Daniel!"

"Why? It's just a kitty cat. It won't hurt me." But, he did stop.

"I'm not sure about what kind of kitty that is." Elizabeth squinted her eyes to make out every detail of the little creature. "I'll wait right here and watch him. I need you to go inside and ask Mom to come out, but to be quiet so we don't frighten it away."

"Why me?" Daniel whined. "Why can't you go get Mom?"

"Daniel!" Elizabeth used her best bossy voice, which meant, "Get your bottom inside and get Mom because I said so! Because I'm the oldest!"

Elizabeth inched toward the little cat to see it better. It was tan-colored with sharp pointed ears and pointed cat-teeth. Curious, it looked at Elizabeth and then raised its top lip and emitted a guttural snarl that came out perhaps less frightening than he would have liked. Elizabeth giggled at his attempt to frighten her. Now, if he were bigger, she thought, he could really scare me!

"What have we here?" Mom whispered, arriving, even with Daniel, so quietly until Elizabeth didn't hear them.

"See the little cat peeking out of the bottom of the cedar tree?" Elizabeth pointed at the little tan bundle who was now deciding to sit in plain sight outside the sweeping branches of the tree.

"Yes," Mom said. "I'm sure it's a little wildcat – or bob cat. It looks like its tail is short. And I know his mom is just like me. If he ran away from her, she's pretty frantic and will stop at nothing to find him. Let's get closer and see if he will let me touch him. He might be able to tell that I'm a mom to you two, just like his mom is to him."

Mom led the way with her hand stretched out toward the little guy. So far he hadn't moved.

Daniel couldn't resist. He simply had to talk to the kitty. "Hey, Bobby," he cooed just above a whisper. "Hey, little guy. Do you like your name? It's Bobby, because you have a bob-tail."

Elizabeth joined in. "Hi, pretty boy," she whispered as they reached the kitty. "You're okay. You're going to be just fine." She looked at Daniel and whispered in a huff to him, "So you've already named him Bobby, huh? What about me? Do I have any say in naming him?"

"Shhh," Mom warned.

Daniel reached toward the cat and he shied away, taking several steps backward out of Daniel's reach. "Oh, he doesn't like me," Daniel said, turning sad eyes toward his mom.

"You just frightened him," Mom whispered. "You must move very slowly and act calm. No loud noises, either."

Daniel sat Indian-style on the ground right in front of the little bob-tailed cat. Elizabeth followed, squatting instead of sitting. Mom was the last to drop to the kitten's space. She knelt, remaining on her knees as she spoke soothing words.

In a move that all three would long remember, the kitty crawled on his belly from behind the sheltering limbs straight into Daniel's lap.

"Stay still, Daniel," Mom said.

The little cat turned his head and looked at Mom. He then looked over at Elizabeth. He must have decided he liked his new family because he burrowed deeper into Daniel's lap and curled up with his nose against Daniel's shirt just above his waist.

Daniel nor Bobby made much protest when Mom stood and then leaned down to gently pick up the baby kitty. She held him against her chest so he could feel her heart beat. That lulled him as she held him close.

They all walked back to the screened porch and Mom said, "Elizabeth, you haven't held him, yet. Sit in the swing and I'll hand him to you. Be careful not to jostle him and he may stay asleep."

"Aw, Mom. I wanted to hold him," Daniel griped.

"You already have. It's now Elizabeth's turn." She looked at the screen door which was opened slightly. Just open enough for a little kitty cat to get through. "Daniel, you'd be a big help if you'll latch the screen door so when he's ready to get down he can't get outside." She turned to open the sliding glass door into the house. "And come into the kitchen with me and we'll warm a little milk and see if he's hungry. He might like it. And I need to see if I can find where he came from so we can get him back to his mommy."

"But I want to keep him, Mom!" Daniel sulked with his bottom lip poked out.

"Shhh. I understand, Daniel. But you wouldn't like to be lost and then found by some big animal who decides to keep you instead of returning you to your family, would you?"

Daniel grinned. "I don't know. At least I wouldn't have Elizabeth telling me what to do all the time!"

"Oh, Daniel, you're too much." His mom laughed and swatted at his bottom with a dish towel.

Soon the fresh milk was heated just enough to take the coldness out of it. Mom took it out of the microwave and opened the door to the porch. Daniel carried it carefully and tried so hard not to spill it. Just as he reached the swing and Elizabeth with Bobby in her lap, he sloshed the milk over the side of the bowl and it dripped onto Elizabeth's bare knee.

"Daniel!" Elizabeth hissed. Then she realized it wasn't even hot and instead of being angry, she grinned at him. But the commotion had awakened Bobby and he stirred in Elizabeth's lap. Daniel set the milk down and gently picked up the baby kitty and set him on the floor by the shallow bowl of milk, not quite as full now as it once was.

The baby stuck his nose in the milk and jumped back in surprise. He sneezed and cleared the milk from his nose. Elizabeth and Daniel exchanged glances and smiles. He tried again. This time his little pink tongue flicked out and he stuck it in the milk. It must have tasted good, because his little tongue was almost a blur as he lapped up the milk, swallowing as fast as he could.

Mom stood in the doorway watching him. "Goodness, he was hungry," she said as he turned away from the milk bowl, seeming to have had his fill. He looked through the screen to the back of the yard. Three sets of eyes followed his. He began to cry.

There, standing by the cedar tree, was a large cat. Actually, a big cat! A big cat with black spots on its tan legs, and pointed ears that stood straight up. And a mouth that was open, but not smiling. It showed an alarming number of teeth.

"It's his mom!" Elizabeth cried.

"I don't want him to go." Daniel cried real tears that made his eyes watery.

"I'm sorry for him to go, too, but he must be reunited with his family," Mom said.

"Daniel, will you unlatch and open the screen door, please?" She picked up the baby kitty, placing her hands around his warm, fat little tummy, and held him in front of her as she walked out to the patio. She carefully placed the kitty on the patio stones and hurried back inside.

The baby sat there for a minute (it seemed forever) and cried for his mommy. Suddenly, the big cat started moving, slinking slowly toward the baby, her eyes moving from him to the three people on the porch and back to him. In a final quick dash, the big bob cat reached her baby. She grabbed the ruff of his neck between her teeth and swung around, quickly covering the space between the patio and the trees as she stretched out her body and sped away. The last thing they saw was her bob-tail disappearing into the woods.

"Wow!" Daniel exclaimed. "I can't wait to tell Anthony and Trey when they get back from Disney World that we had a baby bob cat in our yard."

"How about in our house?" Elizabeth added.

"Yeah, they'll never believe that," Daniel agreed. "Going to Disney World isn't as great as this! Now, this is a summer vacation!"

"How much longer is it until school starts?" Mom joked, looking at her marvelous children with a gleam in her eye.

All three burst out laughing, each letting off a little tension after holding a wild animal close to his heart, with a mama cat out there looking for him. Mamas always find their babies.

That was proved today. Both kids knew that if they were lost, their mom would find them.

Elizabeth hugged her mom and went back to Black Dress Barbie.

Daniel decided he'd read a book inside for a little while. Just in case the baby kitty's mom came back.

Short Story

Finalist Judge – Jenny Jeffers, Tallahassee, Florida

First Place

Coat of Many Faces

Alice Cappa –Monticello, Florida

Six Hours....

A lone horseman galloped through the wood barely ahead of the coming storm. Tree branches whipped wildly across his mount's neck and in a moment, fat cold raindrops would follow. Exhilarated with the wind and the speed of his ride, Wilbro would reach the homestead in a fervor of excitement.

"I see you," he called through the wind to the devic forces whirling around him. A silvery light sparked to his left and a scurry of tiny feet raced out of his path, jumping behind a handy oak. "I hear you!" Tiny wings flapped hurriedly beside his right ear and were gone. "I'm with you," he called.

The Summer Hills' winds caught the thundering hooves, the excited calls, the whoosh of a bird's flight and swirled them high throughout the forest. Magnified beyond reasonable range, sounds carried across treetops, mountain tops, and down into The Hollow to the homestead. The natural verve of the Summer Hills was at its highest in a storm. And this was a "power storm," coming at the height of an ecliptic cycle. Power storms amplified nature. The energy was deep, lingering in The Hollow, blowing down the twisted forest trails, soaking deeply into fibrous tissue and pushing all growth in the Summer Hills to quicken. It lasts but half a day -- five or six hours, tops, then blows away 'til the next cycle. Acting as a conduit to the eclipse itself, the storm dispersed energy to all who would use it. And it must be used!

For Wilbro, his creativity exploded: ideas, strategies, projects. For him, who depended on the aid of the "little ones" for his work, the energy must be solidified to a tangible goal. Once started, though not necessarily completed, his plan must be crystallized before the storm ends, or Wilbro's connection to his creative spirit would be severely curtailed. And as a village elder, his efforts were pivotal in helping the village progress. To ground inspiration to a tangible goal and thrive.

In the calm of The Hollow on this early spring morning, Joscelyn's hearing perked with the first gust blowing in across the frosted meadow.

The energy in The Hollow is bustling this morning.

Humming. Dry grasses waved and squirrels sprinted, waiting to receive the storm from the hills.

And it is "green."

A wintergreen crispness, stripping dead leaves from winter-barren trees, animating sluggish sap within, sweeping down from the forested hills in such a rush as if to scream, "Wake Up!" to the valley below. She went to Granya working in the sheepfold and informed her the storm was bringing a rider from over the mountain.

In her mind's eye, Jos flashed on her brother, his wild silver-red hair flying with the wind, his expression enlivened with the storm.

He's back!

"His trip must have been aborted," Granya said. "Clear the studio for him."

Muffled rumblings beat erratically in time with flashes of light in the clouds, and the darkened sky sunk closer. Inside, Jos lit a fire in the hearth, then swung the small pot of water on its chain over the coals to simmer. She straightened the studio, then watched quietly from the porch for the rider soon to appear. Her yellow chambray smock fluttered over her coveralls with the growing wind while she uneasily twisted the ring on her middle finger 'round and 'round.

Storms were not troubling in The Hollow, though they could significantly alter the land. This storm would be one of the most memorable throughout all the Summer Hills. It held something very uncommon, and Joscelyn was not sure yet what kind of energy was building.

With the arrival of this new tempest, emerged Wilbro, sliding in from a full gallop in a scatter of pebbles and divots. Wilbro, an artist who worked with dyes and fibers, was just returning to the Summer Hills after a noticeable absence. Quick with a smile and a gallant bow, he was often mischievous and playful. Vaulting from his grey gelding while winds whipped through his own grayish hair along with the horse's mane and tail, Wilbro excitedly spun 'round to face the others.

"Don't you feel it?" he cried above the rising roar of the storm. "The energy. So forceful! Don't you see the possibilities?"

He ruffled Jos's strawberry blond curls, swung Granya off her feet with a welcoming laugh, then looked around, ready for two big bear hugs. "Where are the kids?"

"With Dalen on a supply run to the village. And what of your own supply trip?"

"I found what I needed at the guilds and saw no need to stay for the revelry. The yarn colors teased me and the muses pulled me home." Wilbro always spoke of "the vibes" and "the muses," and when he got the right ones together, his work was truly incredible.

"All along the mountain path I see eyes peeping out from behind wind-lashed hawthorns, smiles dancing across torrented streams, and wee footprints sliding beneath the sodden mayapples," he exclaimed. "The little ones are awake indeed!" And then, a sudden thought and a firm decision... "I must create something. In their honor."

Joscelyn and Granya knew Wilbro referred to those tiny devic sprites, plant pixies and rock gnomes said to live in these hills. Although Wilbro was himself known by villagers as "that little one who weaves in The Hollow," to him "little people" were another type of people all together.

"I will create a coat!" he exclaimed, handing Jos the reins of his prancing horse. "A magnificent coat!" A swooshing wind curled around him, as though nodding its approval, brisk, clear, minty. He suddenly became quiet and focused, straightening his skewed cap, and methodically collected his dyes, implements, and new yarns from his satchels. He grabbed his large hand-tooled saddlebags and leaving the horse for Joscelyn to tend, he hurried for the studio within.

Granya and Joscelyn just looked at each other and smiled. Another deep plunge into the well of creative pursuits. And Wilbro's plunges were deep.

Five Hours....

Indoors the wind muffled to a softer tone and the fire crackled quietly. Wilbro paused a moment in reflection.

How to start?

Within his pocket his long, nimble fingers touched his special token.

He slid the old monocle out of its chamois sleeve and recalled his grandfather. He'd been a small elfish man with a copper-colored beard pointing to his waist. Memories of walking with him through the courtyards and arches of the village surged through Wilbro and he felt the big, rough craftsman's hand encasing his own small boy's hand. Where or when, Wilbro could not now recognize. He only saw the images: brick pavers at their feet, whitewashed two-story shops and lofts, wrought-iron curls. Cottages displayed every imaginable flower at their gate, every bud colored with rainbows, trailing off the balconies, crawling up the trellises. Rich textures of stone and petals and multi-fiber rugs of jute, sisal, and wool covered every doorstep. Here he first noticed colors, sparking his love for fiber. Here was the inception for his craft. Lost in memories, he dwelled on inspirations from places long past.

But the monocle was not for everyone's eye. It held a special vision to lend to those who truly observed, truly saw the depths and synchronicities of life around them. Wilbro lifted it to his eye, matching its lens to his own, and at once was transported. With the strength of his own imagination and the magnificent vision of the monocle, he was transported beyond the cottage roof, beyond the cottonwoods and meadow grasses whipping in the wind, beyond the horizon of The Hollow's woods, to soar above the highest ranges in the chain of Summer Hills. His vision tunneled narrowly from the highest pinnacle, filtering the light and clarity to focus on the wet patchwork of hills and valleys below.

A ceremonial coat. A coat to anchor the storm's energy to ritual and progress for the village. How?

Faces peered back at him. Widening smiles under shrubby canopies. Winking eyes beneath the dripping vines. His own image reflected in a pond.

Faces everywhere. Ah, yes.

Of course. But time was passing and he must get started. In a heartbeat his attention was back before the hearth. He carefully returned the monocle to his pocket.

Four hours....

A sharp gust shook the mullioned casement window, pushing through to wave a small spider's web on the inside corner. The loosened latch allowed wet spray within.

With his supplies always ready when inspiration struck, Wilbro now laid them upon the long center table in the studio's wide workspace. From his bag he pulled scraps of fabrics, dyes, various needles, colored threads and trims. A small frame-loom and sketching materials also bulged from the side pocket. He mumbled to himself as he spread items about. "The burlap and wools. No, no. Smooth, must be smooth. Need the dye mordants, too."

Granya arrived and helped prepare the materials and offered the many yarns she herself had spun. "You ply your craft so seriously. But go ahead. Use the storm."

"Seriously?" Wilbro was completely nonplussed at her observation. "My craft is my celebration!" He winked. "But I only have so much time left."

"Yes. Use it. The energy is strong and the regenerating hills need more help." Granya smiled and left him to his own.

All that morning the storm raged, transforming the mountains yet again from their former benign, though barren faces, to freshly rugged ones. And all that morning Wilbro feverishly worked, testing colors and fibers together, weaving, stitching, trying patterns this way and that.

"Too bright? No, brighter. Oh, values don't mesh. Here. No, that one turned...." His muttering further accentuated his thoughts. "Ahhh, you will love this coat, Li'l Ones, but you must give me time." Time. He didn't like his efforts to be matched to a ticking clock, but today there was no choice. With a quick glance he checked the storm's progress outside the window, then turned back to his work. He never saw the water pooling on the floor.

Three hours....

Steady rains pattered at the window panes.

Brightly colored beads lay atop dark, thickly woven swatches. Dye lot samples from roots, berries, and leaves rested experimentally against skeins of cottons, linens, and silks. The scents of cedar wood and fennel still clung to some most recently dyed. Wide swaths of soft fabrics in shades of honey, brick, and pale plum wine were stretched across the benches. His hand accidently brushed aside some silver beads onto the cloth.

Oh! A little sparkle here? Yes?

Yes.

With long dexterous fingers Wilbro manipulated his tools expertly. With every thunder-boom his creations grew stronger and shouted for attention. With every quiet spray of raindrops against the window glass, they softened with more subtle appeal. Wilbro recognized long ago that the flavor of energy that surrounded him as he worked affected his style, and consequently, the finished pieces. His plan for this coat must be perfect, with rich hues unmatched and details just so. Wilbro made several templates, but not one was yet right.

Hurry now. Must keep pace with the storm. If I lose it, I will fail them.

(And myself.)

He picked up his speed with renewed intensity, his eyes glistening and his face working as much as his hands.

Two hours....

A deafening thunderboom rocked the house from without, when Wilbro with great flourish and emphasis pressed bright accent yarns into the weft. The plan was coming. The patterns were pleasing. "For your bright smiles, bright eyes, Li'l Ones. I can't fail you now." But an inner voice unexpectedly questioned the pace of the storm. Time was running out....

Wilbro reached for his shuttle when suddenly a blast of the storm slammed through the loosened window and swirled inside. Wilbro's yarns flew into a spiral, upsetting his patterns and filling the room with a cyclone of color. He looked up aghast.

Noooooo!

Quickly, tensely, he rushed for the window and banged it shut, latching the hook securely. Turning back, he surveyed the damage.

No. No.

But it was done. Tools, swatches, dyes, yarns and templates lay everywhere.

His sequencing and detail destroyed. Wilbro quietly began putting the room back to order, but he greatly feared he'd lost his momentum, his inspiration, his fortitude. Time was an issue and it was almost gone.

Yet he rallied, attempting to recreate his ideas and re-order the patterns already completed. His hands moved swiftly now. Shaping, stitching, weaving. Eyes focused on the work before him; ears remained on the storm outside.

A swoosh of wet leaves brushed the window, blowing the raindrops away. And then, it stopped. Not a movement within or without.

Silence.

Wilbro jerked his head up and waited, worried. Hands poised above his templates, ears straining for any sound, Wilbro waited.

Nothing.

No wind, no rain, no roll of thunder. Was it over? So soon?

Multitudinous expressions crossed Wilbro's face. Wide-eyed surprise, tension, open-mouthed abandonment. Even fear? Color drained from his cheeks and brow. "Nooooooooo."

He deflated to the floor, totally despondent.

Granya appeared framed in the doorway, checking the sudden turmoil and ensuing silence. Seeing his ashen face, startled at his reaction, she gently chided him, "Wilbro, it's okay. You will create again."

"Nooooo. You don't understand. It's theirs. It's part of the storm. If I fail to finish, they will never come to me again. Once started, the plan must be completed or their energy is withdrawn."

"Come now. Are they such taskmasters as you claim?"

"They are resolute."

Granya dropped her gaze. She was worried, too. The Summer Hills had been in decline and all the village residents felt its energy waning. All were dependent....

Was this a challenge? Do I dare to be as creative as the muses above? As the forests and hills? But they inspire me so.

In his mind, Wilbro absolutely knew that if he did not honor the storm and the muses, his work would suffer and consequently, the family, too. I can't fail the family either.

I must not fail the forces of these hills. If I do, they will fail us: our crops, our creations, our livelihoods...

He didn't want to dwell on that further.

He looked up.

Granya looked up.

Waiting. All benefited on the proper use of an ecliptic storm's energy. As said, use it or lo....

Like a gigantic flashbulb popping, a blinding light filled the room while simultaneously thunder cracked directly over the roof. Rain drummed hard on the slate above and the window glass streamed wet again. Wilbro breathed out his relief. He jumped up with a renewed onslaught of creative energy and went at it once more. Granya let him be.

One hour....

Wilbro considered his array of patterns. Five he now had, one per hour he'd been working. Surely, there must be an answer among them, the perfect combination of unusual detail and tactile impressions, of shapes and tints to please the most disarming of sprites. And there was.

Wilbro grabbed the dyes from his first pattern, placed them next to the beads of the third pattern, and topped with the sparkle of another. Dark threads of the deeper template balanced the pale ones of the last. Wilbro was aware now the winds were dying and splashes on the window glass had ceased. The storm was over. And he had his plan.

The storm changed many faces of the mountain that day and duly spent, it softly rolled on down the valley. Wilbro too, spent but triumphant, gathered his supplies and prepared to follow the storm out of The Hollow. As he made ready his horse, he said, "I will put these samples together and bring back my finished creation tomorrow."

Joscelyn nudged Granya as they stood in the doorway and pointed to the colored ribbons still trailing from his saddlebags. She spoke of her amazement regarding his talents. So varied. So vividly colored. And richly tactile, with a strong presence that begged for touching.

Or...translucent yardage, soft and ethereal. Almost intangible, well nigh invisible. His work affected each viewer so personally. And Granya too, commented that his ideas often changed midstream, diverted, refocused. An elfin focus, she was sure.

"Ah that, yes," Wilbro replied, "It amazes me too. But the muses are always with me and my materials ready at hand, no matter what kind of energy arises. But the final form will change. Every time. I must let the form change." He smiled enigmatically for he knew that his hands and his tools expressed an energy that swept down from the hills, colored the valley and enlivened The Hollow. It never failed to inspire him.

The coat that was brought to them the next day was resplendent. It had many brocaded fibers mixed with overshot threads of a fine satin weave. Tiny gemstones outlined pockets, hems and a hood. An inner neck lining of finely tinted lace was as soft and sheer as a gossamer web. Rich, gleaming colors accented woven faces, peeping out from under collars and cuffs or within folds. Faces, yes, for those revealed at the height of the storm. Stitched, painted, molded...alive!

It was a ceremonial coat, some would say a magical coat, conjured up in the exquisite energy of the storm. It would join other power storm emblems in the Village Hall, an inspiration and an anchor, for the town's prosperity. A reminder: pay attention when the winds blow through the hills and scream, "wake up!" Wilbro was pleased; he'd fulfilled the storm's promise. It was vibrant and dynamic. Sometimes it appeared, as Wilbro modeled it this way and that, the eyes followed you, the smiles quickened, a face slightly turned and winked. It was a wonderful coat.

A coat of the little people, for the little people. By surely one of their own.

Second Place

Old and Gooder'n Gold

Lyla Ellzey – Tallahassee, Florida

I am lonely, but I'm too stubborn to admit I need anyone in any way. My husband passed on to his great reward and his home in the sky several years earlier. We had three children, two of whom became successful in their careers. The other? Well, not so much. Now, my bossy son and my daughter are grown and are treating me as if *I* am the child. They think they know what I want before I do. They are certain they know what is best in all cases involving me. Since they know what is best for me, they don't need my input in making any decision *for* me -- ranging from what kind of toilet paper would best serve my hemorrhoids to declaring I should no longer drive. Do they honestly believe I can't tell the difference between Charmin and the lower priced sandpaper that passes for toilet tissue? Do they truly think me to be the menace of the highways?

Each time either of my offspring mention the retirement communities or assisted living facilities, or even the over-fifty-five apartments, I poke my lip out and yell "NO!" with a stomp of my foot for added emphasis. These homes for the elderly are springing up like mushrooms after a soaking rain all over our small city. I hated them all on sight.

What right do my children have to declare me elderly and want to stick me in a home? Heck, I've been surviving quite nicely by myself. I cook. I clean. I entertain. I'm not ready to be elderly.

Then the day came when my son took the final step in seeing I went to a home. He kidnaped me and took me there. By himself. The captive and captor encounter went like this:

"But, I don't want to be old," I whined. "I don't want to give up my house. Or my car. I don't *want* to live with those old people!"

"Now-now, Mom," my son, David, soothed. "You're going to love Winchester Acres. You'll have your own apartment and they'll provide transportation to anywhere you want to go."

"That's what I mean," I yelled. "I'm happy here. I don't want to go there!"

"Sure you do."

"No, I don't -- and I'm not going." Stubbornness was a long suit of mine.

"Yes, you are."

"You can't make me." I said this with what I intended to be a haughty look down my nose at him. It's a tad bit difficult to look down one's nose when the person being looked at is much taller. I shot him the best superior look that I could muster, given the circumstances.

"Oh, yes I can," he said with a glint in his eye and a noticeable lack of a smile.

My first born rushed me before I could run. Wrapping his arms around my thighs with his face pressed against my abdomen (wasn't he getting just a tad too familiar with his mother), he lifted me from my dug-in stance before the fireplace and slung me across his left shoulder. He walked toward the front door, all the while jiggling me in place across his shoulder, and my face bumped against his butt with every step. My head dangled and I was sure all the blood in my body would run out my nose. And *my* butt was in the air.

"Phew! When was the last time you changed your underwear?"

"I don't wear underwear, Mom. I go commando."

"Well, your rear-end stinks."

With his free right hand, he whacked me a good one on my bottom. "Yours smells like a gallon of powder spilled on it."

"It does not," I huffed indignantly, as we were engulfed in a cloud of powder billowing from beneath my skirt.

Ignoring me as completely as one could ignore a nearly two hundred pound weight on his one hundred-seventy pound frame, he yanked open the car door and dumped me inside the back seat. I landed on my back with my skirt around my waist, my legs bent and waving.

"Mo-oommm, cover yourself," he yelped, almost breaking his neck from twisting his face away so quickly. I'm sure he wasn't traumatized from seeing my virginal white granny panties. I'd like to think not, anyway.

"Your fault, not mine. Now get me out of this car this instant!"

He slammed the door and hopped in the driver's seat. Ziiiippp! The child-proof locks disappeared into the doors. I was his captive. Talk about mad!

I fumed and schemed. I needed revenge.

"You'll regret this. All the inheritance is going to your brother. He may be a little slow. His girlfriend is downright ugly. And he may still live in his own little world in my basement. But, just because he doesn't have a job like you, his big-shot lawyer brother – well, actually, he doesn't have a job at all – bless his little heart. But, he loves his mother! He would never put me away like this."

"Can it, Mom. You're being melodramatic. Arthur wouldn't know what to do with an inheritance if it sat in his lap and fiddled "Yankee Doodle Dandy." Your money, the inheritance you're talking about, is going to pay for your meals, your apartment, and upkeep on everything, including you."

"Me? What you talkin' about, Willis?" Looking at him in the rearview mirror, I gave him my best chin-jutting, frowny-face.

"They're going to haul your butt to exercise classes, swimming classes, all kinds of classes and activities, and you *will* participate."

"I can't participate because I'm not going to be there."

"Mom, you're driving me crazy. You *are* going to live there. We've already got everything ready and the papers are signed."

"I'll escape."

"It's not an institution, Mom. There's no such thing as escaping from there."

"Then I'll run away."

"Do I have to hire a keeper for you? Because I will. Someone who's with you all the time. You can't even go to the toilet without her being right there watching you."

"Nobody's ever invaded the privacy of my toilet. Not even your father; God rest his soul. The first person I catch watching me will get his head stuffed in the toilet and my toe inserted where the sun don't shine."

"We're here."

I peered out the window at a grand building, sort of shaped like the Taj Mahal – at least what I thought the Taj Mahal would look like, having never been there even though I asked over and over again to go to India to see it and my tightwad husband refused, saying something about poverty. Come to think of it, whose poverty? Did he mean *our* poverty or the people who spent all their money to build such a place? Never did quite understand that.

David released the locks and helped me out, tugging my skirt down before my feet even hit the sidewalk. I slapped his hand away. "Stop it."

"Well, aren't you just the most delicious thing!"

"What?" I looked to my right. There stood a tall, handsome, dignified gentleman beaming at me through his gloriously thick mustache, his false teeth shining.

"It's providence that brought such a ravishing creature to share our humble abode." He lifted his black and green plaid tam and swept it before him as he bowed deeply to me. He continued the swoop to include the right wing of Winchester Acres.

I stood there with mouth agape until he took my hand in his and tucked it over his arm. He began to lead me into the Taj Mahal look-alike.

"What are you hanging around for?" I said to David. "Go on; get out of here. Scat!"

Third Place

Ghost of Rhody Al

Jan Baross – Portland, Oregon

I'm from Oklahoma, born and bred. Used to own the only gas station in our little town so when you drove in, I was the first hand you'd howdied and shook.

If I'm gonna be honest with y'all, and I am, my yarn ain't just about Rhody Al, what I call the boy now that he's dead. It's about our friendship that had too short a run.

Stirs up a sadness in me that pools into lonely if I let it set too long. So y'all come on up on my porch, settle yer weary nethers and I'll start my story at the beginnin', otherwise my mind jus' won't hold the pieces together.

Can't say as to why I pitched myself over here to Oregon so late in life. Maybe a fresh view 'fore I kicked the bucket, 'cause of the accident. Live grand as I can off social security and the insurance settlement. 'Nuff said on my account.

You can help me by picturin' a silver gray night, moon clouds over my saggin' porch, log house too. Got it on the cheap and I just keep on bein' cheap.

So, me and Al, we used to sit on my porch most every night, rockin' in my rockers, 'cause we was neighbors and I always had enough whiskey in my cupboard for two lonely bachelors. I liked to drink enough to clear my mind of longins' and make everythin' seem jus' about possible.

Picture me as any man's scarecrow in clean dungarees. And here's Al for yer imaginin'. He's what they call dog ugly. Big brown eyes swimmin' behind glasses thicker 'an a barn door, skin so white and splotched, looked like his mama spilt coffee on him, hair dark red as a dyin' rose. It was his brain got all the gifts. He was one of them computer geniuses that loved country life. We had that in common.

Not one to hide his light, Al would lean back in the rocker and holler at the moon. "I get paid more than movie stars! I think thoughts no one ever thought before!"

Them thoughts was suppose to be secret. He said. But when we boozed, he out louded 'em 'cause I was the best friend a secret could have.

"You don't understand a word I'm saying, do you, old man?" said Al.

He meant it kindly. And rightly so. I didn't understand a single word.

One day his computer boss told him to stay home and relax. "We need time to develop your innovations," Al said he said.

I was happy as a hog in mud heaven. Get to use up my useless days and nights with my good buddy Al. Thank you, Lord!

But Al got so bored tryin' to relax he drunk up my whiskey and throwed his skinny computer 'cross the yard like a silver Frisbee trying to bulls-eye my squawky hens.

Since I was old enough to be his pappy, I gave him a stir. "Son, you need a hobby like my wood turnin'. I make useful whistles outta hunks of cured timber."

Al seemed to take my words to heart. Early the next morning I seen him drive off in his big old truck.

I started to worry when I didn't see hide-n-hair of him the whole week-end.

Toward sunset, his truck rolled in haulin' a trailer filled with the prettiest flowerin' bushes I ever seen. Rhododendrons. Young ones, some middle-aged, all of them bloomin' like a Saturday night smile.

Al was grinnin' too. "God Bless America!" he hollered, clearly moved by his own purchases.

This happy boy was not the glum Al I drunk with this past year. His big white teeth was total strangers to me. The feller I'd gotten to know was a button-down stiff with a mapped-out mind and the most cantankerous disposition this side of Perdition. His hard friendship was a song I'd never write. Then, no warnin' to me, he just got hisself all melted-down and open hearted about this particular kind of flowerin' beauty. And it come at just the right time in his life, like these things do.

"Borrow your shovel?" said Al.

Not that he knew one solid bean about what he was doin'. April's good for plantin' so I offered to help. Al didn't pay me no never mind, just started right in. Planted a big white blossomed beauty with burlap roots bulgin' like a fat butt. He called her Big White Bertha and she took some hard diggin'.

Weeks went on by. I watched my boy roof over his loamy acre with Rhodys butted right up to the back porch of his ranch style. He surrounded Big White Bertha with bright red, pink, orange and frilly yellow friends. Hand-sized blooms planted close enough to be stroking' each other with sisterly love.

Al fertilized them gals' roots, strung a waterin' system and spoon fed 'em grainy plant treats. I swear I heard Big Bertha yum-yummin' over those happy extras he thrust into her plump soil.

I sat on my porch watchin' Al work and sweat, day and night, catch his breath, slap his muddy gloves against his muddy trousers and stare at his Rhody gals like them blushin' beauties was pink-faced virgins on a Grange hall dance floor.

He was somethin' to behold.

'Course I missed his skinny ass sittin' on my porch. Woulda hollered him over, but y'all don't get between Al and whatever peak he's climbin'. The only time I did, Al had been paintin' his house for days. I knew, sure as my dog pisses on the same tire every time, when the rains come, the paint would peel.

So I tapped him on the shoulder neighborly to tell him so.

Well, Al turned and blinked slits. A rage in the swim of his eyes. I stepped on back, right into his paint bucket. I just kept steppin' on backwards, flailin' like a caught chicken in the fisthold of a hungry tramp.

I never ever got between Al and his mountain tops again. No sir.

Weeks passed on by. Month for sure. Weather seemed headed for a good run at summer, turnin' warm as a pocket peach.

Nights, I sat on my porch alone with a half drunk bottle. Y'all know what that's like, feelin' bottom heavy lonesome, lead brained and empty hearted, like to die 'cause yer tired and there ain't no point. Yep, any bozo says they ain't never been that lonely is a lyin' fool. Least ways I just kept on, watchin' the boy musclin' that mulch.

My heart never did hold a sweet spot for somethin' useless as flowers. But that blanket of Rhody colors brought on recallin', me sittin' close to my Mama's big fat hands, her and her friends in our kitchen quiltin' all the colors of the rainbow.

Back then, Mama's ripped up pieces of cloth was the best colors in my world.

Footsteps! Someone was comin' fast, but I was too lit up to move. I trusted in the Good Lord, figured maybe it was Al closin' in with a sweet will. Sure enough, after makin' the most damned beautiful Rhody garden this side of God's creation, it was me he come to rest beside.

He plopped his muddy bottom on the chair and filled a glass full.

"Whaddaya think of my hobby now?" Al said, first words in a month.

"Done good, boy," I said.

"I brought you a present," he said. He handed me a dwarf Rhody, like them little people on TV only legless and not really a person. The little pink bush face was tilted up at me like it was honing for a daddy. I knowed when I been adopted, so I planted Little Tilda, what I called her, by the steps where I could water her easy and she could watch the goings on.

Al and me got back to our fine tradition of drinkin' buddies again. Thank you, Jesus. Time was gonna pass slow and quiet again, just like I liked it.

I wasn't happy he brought his banjo to our little party. He said he'd written a song for his Rhody gals and started in singin'. Whiniest voice in the world.

"Alpenrose! Asterid! Azaleastrum!"

Lord, help me. I sighed like a signal. But he kept on plunkin'.

"Wait until you hear the subgenus!" said Al. "There's 20,000 hybrids and I can sing all their Latin handles!"

"Prunifolium! Calendulaceum!...."

I was all sighed out and he weren't no nearer the end. But, like family, good with the bad. I heard him out.

'Bout a month later some magazine folks drove out and took pictures of his garden. Al couldn't a beamed prouder. People come from three states away 'cause of that article.

Getting' older, I'm more easily irritated. I ain't ashamed to say it. I hate folks treadin' through my idle life. Surely don't want 'em millin' next door.

Matters got worst 'cause them computer folks called Al, ready for some more genius stuff. The news lit him up.

"See you, old man," said Al. Shiny new Apple under his arm.

I drunk alone. First week was the toughest. Second week he shuffled on over with the biggest grin on his face I'd ever seen.

"I'm in love," he said. "I think."

Cleo fixed the computers at Al's work. Al didn't know them rules about not likin' women who was better than men at things men was supposed to be better at. Seeing as how she was some kinda wild weed and seeing as how he was too, they'd clumped together quick like weeds do.

Cleo was older than Al and angry-as-hell MEAN. Weekends them two was a fright. Cleo pushed Al to the wall. He sprung back like a wounded grizzly. I hoped he wouldn't do too much harm and she wouldn't do too much harm, and the harm they did or didn't do each other would balance out at the end of the night. Least ways, they'd always ended rollin'. Lots a lovin', lots of loud lovin'.

I'd put candle wax in my ears and sometimes couldn't barely get it out in the mornin'.

Once in a while, Al snuck over to my place for a drink after he and the lady was done. She'd see us and yell for him to get home and he'd high tail it. I wanted to ask him why he needed a wild weed in his life. They got a talent for stranglin'. I figured probably she broke his cherry and he was grateful. Bein' green at love, he didn't know no better, that you could have a bed-crazy woman under you who treated you kindly after.

But I ain't one to talk. Women chewed me up and hawked me out like used up tobacco. There was one mighty sweet gal. But that's a different story, same regrets.

A month into the marriage Cleo gave Al a loud ultimatum that I couldn't help but overhear.

"You sell this dumb house next to that dumb neighbor. We're moving to the suburbs to raise our babies!"

Al loved his bride and he loved his Rhodys. But ultimatums make a man slow.

When Cleo moved across town, Al finally started packin'.

That hit me harder than I can tell you. I was countin' on Al to find my dead body when I give it up. Him workin' the whisky glass out of my clenched fist an buryin' me with some solemn regrets at my passin'. But him leaving me now -- like a son dyin' before the pappy.

Al took Polaroid pictures of every single bush, every single bud to bloom. Filled three shoeboxes with snaps. Left me a Polaroid of himself with his favorite, Big White Bertha. I took the picture and hung it in my kitchen.

"Watch over my Rhodys, old man," said Al.

"Sure," I said, my heart tighter than a bull knot. "I ain't the one leavin'."

Didn't mean to say it accusin', but I was pained just then.

Al jumped into his big black truck. Engine's hard roar was as much of a goodbye as I got.

I watched the noon dust settle after his tires was gone. And then it kinda got dark, like I was goin' blind faster than I was goin' blind. And damned if my hearin' didn't take a dive. Or maybe it was just too quiet with Al gone.

I figured he'd be back to water and weed, but he never did come. It's serious when a man loses the will to weed.

From sitting' quiet on the porch, my eyes come normal after a time. I watched Al's Rhody gals shrink under the weight of blackberry bushes. Rhody blossoms glowin' like panther eyes set deep in a dark jungle.

Al still hadn't sold his home. That gave me hope.

The boy showed up one late afternoon. I was so happy to see him I could barely swallow my spit.

He sat there on my porch like old times. But it weren't like old times. He drunk too fast and without a joy, holdin' onto a small sign that said his house was for sale.

I nailed it out there on the road for him on account he just couldn't.

A middle aged woman, a sturdy woman, bought his house. She was too much the lady to drink with me. She was strong as a horse and had an iron will to make things perfect. She cleaned up Al's garden and made the Rhodys blossom into even bigger busted glory. Then she painted the house and the paint didn't peel.

Al come over on some week ends, He watched her from my porch, rockin' back and forth and drinkin' hisself sick. 'Bout midnight he'd stumble into his truck and woved on back to the suburbs. Don't think I didn't worry.

One night after we was two bottles gone, I never will forget. His shoulders started shakin' like he was sick. Never figured on tears, poured outta the boy's sockets like a broken levee. He blew his nose 'til I run outta napkins.

He was slurrin', but the story come out. Cleo was sick of him, his garden blues, his crazy ways. She'd filed for divorce and kicked him gone. He was ripped up fierce.

"Hey, old man, can I stay?" said Al.

I nearly hugged the boy. I told him, sufferin' over a woman passes quick in a man. But friendships, they's all that's worth it. He'd see that soon enough.

We kept on boozin' that night drownin' our private achins', drinkin' way past poison 'til we was knees-up, plastered-to-the-floorboards drunk. I couldn't a moved if the Good Lord ordered it. But Al, he crawled off the porch on all fours draggin' his paws across the yard like a worn-out bird dog after an all night hunt.

Next mornin' I woke gawkin' up at the rotted porch shingles.

I pulled myself into a chair and looked for the boy. Finally saw his thick boots stuck out from under Big White Bertha. He always loved layin' under her lily white blossomed boughs. Said it was like starin' up the skirt of a big fat princess at a fancy dress ball.

So I let him be. Figured the sturdy lady who owned the place wouldn't see him unless she watered him down.

But Al didn't wake up by late mornin', didn't crawl back up on the porch retchin' and beggin' for coffee. Didn't come up for lunch. I guessed he was too sad for company.

I knew better than to interrupt Al. So I let him be.

After dinner, I settled into the porch shadows, called over to him. He didn't answer. I knew my friend was edgin' beyond help.

So I clomped quiet as I could to the garden that was no longer his. Big White Bertha's petticoats had dipped down so Al's boots was almost hid. And some mornin' glories, known for their fast moves, had twinned round his soles.

I bent and shook his boots. Couldn't stir him. The way his legs had stiffened I realized with a jolt that Big White Bertha had packaged up my buddy Al like a mail order catalogue. The boy weren't goin' nowhere.

My gums got a sudden ache. My old heart beat wild as an Oklahoma cockfight.

When I got to breathin' regular again, I wiped my eyes and went to my rocker.

Tried to think how to make this good. A good endin' for Al. And me.

I told myself. Al wasn't really gone. He just traded hisself in, like I did my used-up pick up for the new Ford wagon. A happy upgrade.

That's what I been tellin' myself. I should be glad. Al's at peace with the things he loved best, tucked safe and serene in the virgin boughs of Big White Bertha.

He's the lucky one. He got what I always wanted.

To spend eternity in the golden arms of an ever lastin' love.

Adult Novel Excerpt

Finalist Judge – Rob MacGregor, West Palm Beach, Florida

First Place

Baby Sitters

Suzanne Burns – Bend, Oregon

We loved his hair best of all. How the sun turned the top of his head yellow when he stood on the front lawn to pay us after each babysitting job that summer, staring at his shoes while he handed us money like he almost felt sorry for having feet.

After Mrs. Miller died, and what we deemed the appropriate mourning period of one month, we pooled our money to buy a dozen boxes of dye from Long's Drugs, because loving Mr. Miller was a sacrifice. Our sacrifice.

We sacrificed better money by cancelling any other job if he needed us, which we'd done since they brought the baby home months before. The baby we wanted to be our baby with him, not with her. The baby we wanted to push in a stroller through the park while other women stopped to coo and ahh, and how we would have no time to discuss mom things, like diaper rash and teething rings, because we had to get home to cook Mr. Miller dinner. She cooked for him. We wanted to cook for him, too, only our roast beef really would fall from its bone, our mashed potatoes almost mashing themselves after we learned the secrets. Real butter, whole milk, a ricer we'd have to sacrifice two months of Bonne Bell lip gloss to buy.

Without Mrs. Miller in the house, we sacrificed everything more freely. We sacrificed saving for the new Nirvana CD after all the Rolling Stone magazines in town sold out when Kurt, and we only ever called him Kurt, our other favorite blonde, posed in that field with his torn jeans and his thrift store sweater.

We sacrificed sleep to call each other late at night and dissect, through the accepted static of cordless phones, what we had learned from our latest time spent in his house. Some of us took pleasure in breaking down the profile of his cologne before we even knew the language of scent. Calvin Klein's Obsession for Men, how we dared each other to uncap the brown top and hold the bottle to our noses in his bathroom. Double-dog-dares to inhale the cologne so deeply, and for so long, our heads pounded. The rare triple-dog-dare to spritz his cologne on both wrists, behind each ear. When we inhaled Obsession, a smell, we agreed, somewhere between being embraced by an animal and a man, we knew, even at seventeen, we could be content smelling the cologne, and blessing Calvin Klein, the rest of our lives. Cinnamon and carnations, we argued. No, vanilla and lavender. Burnt. Two of the boys at school wore the same cologne for graduation, but not the way Mr. Miller wore it.

Others scrutinized the metallic, alien objects in his kitchen. A garlic press, a tong to toss salad, a machine that baked bread and another that crushed ice for fruit smoothies.

Was that a waffle iron? On Sunday mornings, before the baby came, did Mr. and Mrs. Miller sit at the small breakfast nook feeding each other thick Belgian waffles doused with real maple syrup?

He still used the coffee grinder she gave him for some anniversary. We marveled at the vague sensuality of a wife giving a husband such an industrial looking love token.

Sometimes, after we grew bored of staring at our reflection in the bread machine, we ran a finger along the silver rim of the coffee grinder, almost as if when we touched an object so intensely personal, a collective blush spread from our fingers through the neighborhood. Without him asking, we moistened paper towels to clean up wayward coffee grounds. Grounds she would have never let blight her kitchen counter.

During the day, when he taught summer term at the college, we fought for which one of us accepted the job of pretending to watch the baby sleep while we fondled her tubes of Lancôme lipstick, Kettle Rose, or made crooked, only to again straighten, the guest bathroom hand towels. Sometimes we tried on her clothes. We made a pact to never spray a golden mist from her bottle of Dune, already dusty on her side of the bedroom dresser.

We didn't mention Madeline Miller, our first suicide, the entire month of June.

Kurt would take his life two years after our neighbor slit her wrists in the downstairs tub where we bathed her son. And she didn't give away any of her possessions first, like Chad Lowe in that TV movie we all watched as children, right after he wrote "Dying is an art" in the margins of every page of a book of Sylvia Plath poems. His suicide note, by default. Maybe Chad Lowe, as Skip Lewis, was our first suicide?

She didn't leave a note. We wondered as we listened to Courtney Love read Kurt's suicide note on TV during his vigil, "Just tell him that he's a fucker, okay? And that you love him," if Mr. Miller watched the way we watched, huddled under our blankets with our new boyfriends whose hair, even the blonde ones, never could compete.

We tried not to think about whether he forgave us for everything that happened before his wife died. None of us meant to get her in so much trouble. We all loved her, too, in our own small town teenage way that turned any woman not born and raised in our county into a worthy rival.

Even with her dead and gone, our favorite opponent in the game of trying to seduce Mr. Miller, though not all of us viewed the game as sport, there was still just something about his hair. Fiona called the color Sunflower, but we disagreed. At the drugstore we all bypassed the make-up aisle, putting on hold our ritual of secretly breaking the seals on as many lipsticks as we could to test each color on the inside of our wrists. We headed in a brunette rush towards the hair color. Some chose Goldenrod.

Others, a shade called Chamomile. Those of us who babysat in the evenings veered towards colors with names like Beeline and Ginger Ale. The lucky few who got to see Mr. Miller in the morning, his hair still damp from the shower as he rushed not to be late for work, agreed on the color Vanilla Malt, each clutching a box as close as we could to the proximity of our teenage hearts.

At one of our houses we broke open the seal on each box to marvel at the contents inside. That summer afternoon no one knew how to define the word talisman, but we hoped the hair dye, all the plastic bottles and the tubes of after-color conditioner and the gloves, so tight and thin our bony fingers split several pairs, would bring us closer to understanding how one house on our block became the biggest scandal the neighborhood still remembers.

We took turns dying our hair Vanilla Malt. Some left on the bleach mixture longer than others, some timed the peroxide processing to the recommended minutes from the fold-out instructions. After all the primping, and the applying of various barrettes, we stood in front of the bathroom mirror, our hair now his hair, our faces almost morphing to resemble his face, a chorus of girls who could either be, at any moment as the vagaries of light from the bathroom window curled under our newly fragile ends, either his lovers, or his daughters.

Fiona stuck with Sunflower but refused to change the color of her hair. "Nothing from a box could ever come close to matching him," she told us, "or her."

Her?

Fiona carried the box with the photo of a dyed blonde shag cut around the rest of the summer. The only girl who got so close to Mr. Miller she called him Tom, as in, even though at school he teaches Writing 121 as Mr. Miller, in the real world he goes by Tom.

"Do you call him Tom when he fucks you?" we asked, but she has refused to tell us, even after all these years.

Fiona carried the box of hair dye around so long, the taped top opened. The contents spilled out and settled in the bottom of her United Colors of Benetton flag purse, the purse we all coveted when she moved to town at the beginning of our Senior year, months before the suicide. Small white bottles lolled inside the designer canvas, out of context among her wallet, her keys attached to a mini pink Koosh ball, the current copy of Sassy magazine with the cover story "Do You Need Armpit Hair to be a Feminist," the one condom she got free from Planned Parenthood the year before when a nurse at a school more progressive than ours demonstrated how to unroll the exotic white sheath on a perfectly erect banana.

She stole her mother's best pinking shears to cut out the picture on the box. With packing tape, she told each of us on the phone at separate times during separate, specific confidences, she covered the picture of a woman with hair dyed Sunflower. Homemade laminating, she called it, to keep the picture safe, to reminisce the color of his hair in her wallet the way parents keep photos of their children.

This made us wonder if Mrs. Miller had time to put a photo of the baby in her wallet before she died. If she cared about things like photos at all, and why did she buy a new tube of Kettle Rose the week before Fiona found her like that, everything around her red while she sort of floated in the center of it, a silent observer with skin so white, Fiona swore she looked prettier than we'd ever seen her. More white than our mothers' bone china. Chiclets, her teeth looked like mint Chiclets beneath her blued lips. So did her fingernails, surrounded by all that red.

Over the years we have chosen different ways to commemorate the moment Madeline Miller stopped existing in her world to become a legend in ours. She did keep a diary of sorts we stole from the house as the ambulance took her away and still pass between us, a little red appointment book where she scribbled down reminders to pick up dry cleaning and buy organic yogurt. She also marked the days each of us babysat, our names written in the sophisticated cursive of an older woman looking almost not like our names. She marked the days she saw her lover with a gold star. We hoped for years she didn't steal the gold stars from Mr. Miller's teaching supplies, though the idea of such a brazen act intrigues us more than it disgusts us as we grow older.

What we don't have are any photos of Mr. Miller, of her lover, of her. This has made memory our historian. One of us can recall her auburn hair. Another, the sort of laughter it's taken two decades to define as nervous to be in the presence of our fingernails, painted Wet' n' Wild 415A, cheap, the only blue-black polish in town, our tips always chipped, and of our Teen Spirit green apple deodorant, and of the way the sun sparked our hair with natural highlights we only now appreciate.

At some of our yearly dinners one of us reads a poem about her, usually a sonnet, though only a few at the table recognize the ending couplet. Others bring drawings. Some haunt the paint aisle of the home improvement stores a week or two before we meet to pilfer samples. White Dove, Frostine, Cloud Cover, nothing ever captures the color of her dying skin. Those of us who live in town drive to the next town over, and next home improvement store past the freeway off-ramp, where no one we know can see us fill our purses with colors like Ablaze and Stolen Kiss and Valentine. We make a game of seeing how many paint samples lined up on paper the size of bookmarks match the color of blood in water.

"Here, look at this one," we whisper to each other. "This is the color."

"No. It's this one."

"Nope. That's the color of the light on the ambulance. This is the color of the water. Not like blood, but not really like anything else."

"Do you remember the last time you saw them together?"

"Mr. and Mrs. Miller?"

"No, Mrs. Miller, Fiona and him. You know."

Each year we reserve the corner table in our favorite restaurant the last Friday evening in June. The ones who fly in still arrive for a pre-dinner cocktail. Years ago we toasted Madeline Miller to Cosmos. The last few years, Lemon Drops, mojitos, maybe one or two chocolate martinis. If we drive, we drive together in our caravan of extended grief. This year we'll reach a milestone some will mark with a bouquet of balloons floating above our table, like this is something to celebrate. The one who takes the sort of photographs a publishing house in New York forms into coffee table books will take even more than usual. The one who became a mom will bring a cake, because this year we are finally the same age as her.

It took us twenty years to catch up to Mrs. Miller. Twenty years to understand how it feels when a nineteen-year-old hostess walks us across the restaurant with her lean calves and no split ends.

Two years ago a hostess with fingernails painted a glittery baby blue sat us, then opened our menus before placing them in our French tipped fingers. The next May we arrived with our nails the same baby blue, only to see a different hostess with an even shorter skirt, her nails painted a maroon so dark, under candlelight they looked black. "We used to paint our nails black, too, or at least almost black," we told the hostess, ashamed as we hid our nails the color of bird eggs under the table. "You should have seen how good our one friend could do it."

"No one really paints their nails anymore." The hostess giggled like we should die from our own stupidity. "They're called gel strips."

We pretended to type the name of her favorite salon into our phones while under the table we clawed our home-painted, out of fashion nails into the flesh of our palms.

This year we will make promises to give up trying to compete with the hostess, whose voracious fertility leads its way around the restaurant like an unacknowledged, yet irresistible, force. We will promise to ignore the study printed in a medical journal with enough plain speak to be picked up by Yahoo News. The "vampire theory" that blood from young bodies may be able to reverse the aging process, something close to touting a cure for Alzheimer's. All those vivacious corpuscles, under a microscope a tango of single cells darkly blushed in hemoglobin's red glow. How we all envy each year what we cannot see beneath the hostesses' skin, and how we wonder if our bodies, pulsing with the hidden secrets of our own aging blood, carried, two decades ago, the ability to make Mrs. Miller feel obsolete, even with a lover who sometimes sat on the front lawn under her cherry tree as she slept, maybe in his mind somehow keeping her safe. From what, we're still trying to figure out.

Each year as our skin loses its elasticity, as our hearts shrink, still imperceptible though we are losing the fight to keep up, we order our steaks more and more rare. At nineteen, our first year to gather at the only restaurant in our small town that offered a choice of rice pilaf as a side, which we considered classy, we only knew to order our steaks well-done. We requested ketchup. But we did ask for rice pilaf before pushing the unfamiliar density of darker grains around on our plates. We tried, and failed, at seeming exotic. We, especially that first year, wanted to hear mouths we did not know pronounce words like "pilaf," foreign to our small town sameness, words to shield us from being known as The Babysitters.

His Babysitters.

At one time, Their Babysitters.

The first summer after Mrs. Miller killed herself we knew what the waiters thought of us by how they either never refilled our water glasses, or hovered around our table with a pitcher at the ready in hopes of snaring any gossip, though the first year we only spoke of what to order, of which fork to use, of how to eat our tough steaks with the least amount of attention placed on us.

Over the years as we piece together what happened between Fiona and Mr. Miller, Mrs. Miller and her lover, our hostess gets younger; first a girl we all went to high school with, then a few years younger than us, then young enough to be our daughters. So our orders slant towards blood to keep up. We consume steaks so red, under the light they shine purple, some cuts so rare the centers feel cool on our tongues. We relish steak Carpaccio appetizers, chewing until the juices bruise our lips. The art historian among us, her mouth full of raw steak, regales us with tales of Vittore Carpaccio, the dish's namesake.

"Whenever you make it to Venice," she says, "you need to see the painting The Dream of St. Ursula."

She never describes the angel who watches the saint sleep or the potted carnation or the small dog waiting as a sentinel next to her bed, or the fact that most of us will never make it to Venice.

Second Place

Dangerous

Kara Imle - Austin, Texas

Prologue

I see movies in my head. Only they aren't movies, because movies aren't real, and only happen on a flat screen in a dark theater.

These movies are all around me. They come from behind and in front and above me. I am in the movie, watching it take place, like a dream, except I can move. Sometimes in dreams I can't move and I am terrified because I can only watch what is happening. Mom always says I'm "spacey," but I'm not spacing out. I'm paying attention to the movies all the time.

My movies are real, as real as the school bus I ride or the chairs I sit on or the trees I climb. There is a dragon that comes from out of nowhere. He crashes through walls and ceilings, or tunnels through the sides of mountains. I think he lives up there, in the mountains, but I don't know. I've never seen his cave. I just think he lives in one because that is where most dragons live.

The world is round and all of us live inside of it. I live in the part where people walk around with their feet down and their heads up, and I like to lie in the grass and look up at the sky, and think about all the people whose heads hang down while their feet are stuck to the inside of the ball. I wonder how they don't fall down, out of the sky? Is my ground their sky? Is that how gravity works?

At night, when I look up at the stars, I think of how they are holes punched in the giant round world we live in, and the bright light beyond is shining through. I would like to get close to a star and look out of it. I wonder what I would see? Are there other worlds out there, or are we the only one? Is there anything out there at all, or just a big empty room with the lights on?

Whose job is it to turn out the lights when it's time for the world to go to sleep?

Pastor Lemon says that God is watching all of us to see if we are sinning or not. He says God can see every person in the world all at the same time, and that He knows all of our thoughts. But how can that be? Where does God live? Is He outside of the ball, peeking into the star-holes? How could He see every single person, even the ones in Africa, even the ones that live on tiny islands, even me, hiding in the woods with my dogs and my dragon?

I think I saw God once. He wasn't an old man with a long white beard like the picture of Him in the Bible. He was dark, like a shadow, and He showed up on the side of a mountain once when I was a very little kid and had just broken my leg learning to ski. I didn't know my leg was broken. I had fallen down, and I was watching my mother get farther and farther away from me.

I was alone. Other skiers swerved around me and disappeared. I tried to get up, but a giant, invisible hand pushed me down and trapped my breath.

"Don't move, stupid," a voice said. It came from all around me. The bright snow turned gray as the inside of a cloud. My dragon was nowhere to be seen. I couldn't move. It was like in a dream, but I wasn't terrified. I wasn't anything. I obeyed, and didn't move. I saw God's back as He drifted away, and the hand lightened and left me. Soon after that, my mother came back.

She picked me up and held me in her arms and skied the rest of the way downslope and found a doctor.

That's how I know there's a God. But I don't think it's the same one Pastor Lemon is talking about. I don't know if he's met this God or not.

But he's met my dragon, lots of times.

~~

Chapter 1: Not An Accident

February is a mean month and I'm in a mean mood. The dark winter days are giving way to longer and longer daylight hours, but not fast enough for my fevered brain. Alaska's seasons give no quarter to those whose psychiatric balance depends upon consistency. The winter darkness drops me into despair, the endless summertime light sends me sky-high, and the in-between stages are a study in feverish impatience, boozy sadness, euphoric energy and searing irritation. This year I am particularly volatile, spring hitting in the midst of an off again/on again romance with a married man I feel karmically bound to, our destinies wound together like threads of a dark tapestry that is coming undone.

I have not slept in many days. I believe there is a stranger stalking my house, and I've been hunting him in the night with a shovel that I keep by my bed. He leaves footprints in the snow that lies deep in my yard, and when I follow them, they only lead around again to the front window. Has he been standing there, watching me? The thought works me into a rage, and when I leave the house to run errands I am already driving angry. I am looking for trouble the way an alcoholic looks for a drink.

Red light. I sit coiled tight as an angry cat in the driver's seat of my 4Runner, knuckles white on the wheel. It is middling cold out, not quite freezing, just the kind of late-February weather in Anchorage that keeps the roads glazed with a frictionless scum of watery ice. "Slicker'n snot," my mother calls it. It's not the ice that's got me wound up, though. It's the stalker, the other people on the road and the world generally that have me twisted. The light turns green, and four lanes of traffic start spinning their wheels for purchase on the dirty, rutted ice. I'm signaling left, and I need someone to let me in but nobody's giving me room. Behind me, in the left-hand lane, I spot a woman in my rear-view. Chevy Tahoe, silver, gunning up to close the gap and block me from turning. She's looking down at her lap, not paying attention to the road. I see her coming and it's like somebody's punched me in the jaw. I often react violently to physical threats. On a different day I might have let it go with a curse and a dirty look, but not today. I'm signaling, and I'm going to turn left goddammit, the intersection is approaching and I'm running out of time.

I clench the wheel, clench my jaw, make a hard left, and sure enough she's got no time to stop. The Tahoe skids into my left rear panel with a percussive crunching sound, tearing off my bumper and pushing both cars forward, locked together like hockey players over a puck, and the traffic behind us piles up in slow-motion.

Time takes a break, and the rage begins to drain away, all the agitation and hatred fizzling out, flattening, uncoiling. My pulse does not race. My gaze unlocks itself from the rearview and settles straight ahead, fuzzing over, seeing nothing but the dashboard. The heat, it seems, is turned up way too high. I reach forward and turn it down. I am calm, insulated, as if a giant airbag has exploded around me and is now holding me in place, although the wreck itself is too mild to have touched off my car's airbags. For a few seconds, nothing happens.

Then here she is at my window, banging on it with her fist, her face a contorted mask of rage, screaming at me. I stare back at her, and feel my lips beginning to twitch into a smile. I've really gotten her pissed and this means that I'm the one in charge. All that rage I was feeling, all the anger and pent-up energy and powerlessness and hyped-up choked-up frustration, I've channeled it straight into this woman. And now she's frothing and hopping outside my car. I watch her for a moment, then press the button that slides the window down.

"...can't just turn in front of someone without looking, I had the right-of-way, why'ntcha watch where the fuck you're going?" She's practically gargling with too much spit, the words tumbling over themselves. She looks like the crazy person, and people are getting out of their cars, coming over to us, asking if I'm okay. She yells a bit more, but I just regard her quietly, my invisible airbag still stuffing the space around me, a cushion of silence. Our slow-motion crash has caused no bodily harm, has barely dented her vehicle though my bumper is dangling off. She looks around, taking in the scene. It looks as if she's rear-ended me and is now screaming at me.

I watch as the light-bulb pings on over her head.

She turns on her heel and slides back to her car, slamming the door hard and loud, like an exclamation point. She guns the engine, hits reverse and then takes her coveted left turn, leaving me with the feeling of an earthquake passing: the I can't believe that just happened moment. I can feel myself beginning to shudder, down deep in my guts.

A few minutes (hours?) later, I am in the parking lot of the grocery store, having a breakdown. I know I am having a breakdown because I physically can't stop shaking. I get out of the car, stand up, and lean on the door for support. My body wavers like a tree in a gale-force wind; or maybe it is my eyes, which cannot seem to focus on any one thing but twitch wildly back and forth. I dig out my phone, call my married lover, tell him what has happened, and ask him to come and get me. I know that our thread is unraveling, but I want him to come. I want him to care about what is happening to me.

"No," he says, full-stop. And, when that sinks in after a moment, "I'm working from home." His home is a few blocks from where I am nervously breaking down in the parking lot.

Rather than beg, fight or explain, I hang up.

Now I am shrinking: my body is actually growing tiny. I have to use both hands and my feet to climb back inside my car, which is now enormous. I hang my midsection over the seat like a child working her way up a jungle gym. This would freak me out, except I am already at maximum freak-out, far from the cool, aloof, dissociated self I presented while the woman screamed at me.

I need help. I use my teensy fingers to dial my friend Matt, because I know he will come even though he is working, has a toddler at home, and any number of projects going on all the time. And I'm right, he is working, but when he hears my voice he drops it all, says, "Hang tight and I'll be there in twenty."

Time telescopes for me, trapped there inside my vehicle, and those twenty minutes stretch into hours. Every time someone walks by I glare wildly, wondering if this person, no maybe that one, or is it him, over there, is HE the one who's been stalking me? Did he follow me here from my house? Is he going to try and kill me now that I'm out here in the daylight, by myself, without my shovel? Growling and muttering, I crouch down behind the wheel and lock the doors. I can barely reach them. I will kill anyone who comes close to the car. I need help. I should go to the hospital. That's what I'll do—when Matt gets here I'll tell him I need to go to the hospital. I will be safe there. They won't let anyone hurt me, and they won't let me hurt anyone else.

~~

Chapter 2: Bright Lights, Beautiful Colors

Marne holds my hand in the ER waiting room, which is kind of her because she's not the hand-holding type and I am very emotional and she is also not the emotional type. No-Name is here, too, which makes it a little easier. I don't know what else to call him. It seems like a good name for a tiger no one else can see. He's been following me around lately, ever since Jacob and I started getting really intense about our relationship. My married lover: the phrase rings in my head all the time, wracked with guilt and pleasure. No-Name's presence keeps me company when Jacob is not around, which is more and more these days. So he's here, and that's comforting because there are people in here who are actually sick, like a kid with a really bad cough, and this other woman vomiting into a pink plastic cup.

I want to die. I mean I don't want anything anymore, really. But if I did want something, it would be that. Not because I want to be dead, but because it seems like the only way to get off the planet. I don't belong here. I'm not from this dimension. When I met Jacob I thought I'd met my fellow traveler—another alien, another being like me, someone who understood the messages Icarus and Prometheus and the others left behind. But he didn't. He journeyed a little way with me and then turned back. I tried to go on alone but the price of flight is very, very high. Ha! No pun intended. That was a good one though.

I twist my arm through Marne's, my heart beating too fast. I don't really know how this is supposed to go. My therapist said, when I called her yesterday and told her about the accident that wasn't an accident, that she'd call ahead for me. But they don't seem to know who I am. The nurse took my name then told me to sit here and wait. Waiting makes me itchy, agitated. No-Name doesn't seem bothered at all, but what does he have to worry about? Who would bother a tiger? He's just lying there with his head on his paws, faking sleep. Like he doesn't notice the people walking around and through him. He could stand up and roar. He could swipe their heads off with the stroke of a paw.

Really, I'm as not-here as he is. My physical body is a projection beamed through a worm-hole in the universe, and my real self, my true essence, dwells in a parallel reality. If I could go anywhere, absolutely anywhere, I'd go to the horsehead nebula. It's so beautiful, suffused with the light of billions of suns. I like to look at bright lights and beautiful colors because they seem to feed a part of my brain that is starving, and I wonder if this is the part where my soul lives. And I imagine my soul is made of gorgeous glowing colors and every time I look at anything beautiful, it aches because it is homesick.

Finally—the nurse is calling my name. Marne pats me encouragingly. I go up to the little cubicle. Triage, that's the word. They do triage to see who has the most urgent need for the doctor. But what kind of doctor am I going to see? I sit down facing her in the little glass cube, our knees touching.

"So?" she says nicely, although tiredly, as if she has asked this question many times already. "What brings you in today?"

I have been practicing this a bit. My therapist told me what to say, but I'm having a hard time with the words. They seem rude, as if someone has just asked if you'd like a cup of tea and you have to tell them well actually, I hate Earl Grey and also, your mother is an asshole. I am stumbling over the phrase, so I try telling her the story of why I am here.

"I got in a car accident yesterday. I'm not hurt. But, it was on purpose. It was a non-accidental accident." The nurse is really looking at me now, as if she's waking up a bit. I'm on the spot, and my thoughts are milling around like mustangs in a pen. I don't know, these days, what will happen when I open the gate. I sigh and say the words.

"I might be a danger to myself," I say.

And a danger to you, I think, remorsefully. The nurse stiffens a bit, backs away from me, so that our knees are no longer touching.

"Are you saying," she asks me slowly and deliberately, "that you are a danger to yourself and others?" I look at my lap and nod. But she asks again. "Are you dangerous to yourself and others?"

I look up, meet her eyes. I think of the moment I turned, hard left, in front of the woman driving up too quickly behind me. I think of the people on the road whose cars piled up behind us. I think of the moment, in an incandescent rage, that I lifted Jacob -- all 6′ 3″ of him -- and threw him across the yard. I think of all the times I've tried to leave the planet. I am exhausted. She's waiting for my answer.

"Yes," I tell her. "I'm a danger to myself and others."

Third Place

Mahmoud's Jihad

Geoffrey Dutton – Belmont, Massachusetts

Part I: Seeking Refuge

We have awoken, and all of creation has awoken, for Allah,
Lord of all the Worlds. Allah, I ask You for the best the day has
to offer, victory, support, light, blessings and guidance; and I seek
refuge in You from the evil in it, and the evil to come after it

Salat al-Fajr

~~

CHAPTER ONE

He had just started walking when a seabird swooped
toward him with a sharp shree, as if to remind him he had
forgotten to do something important. So there, in a chill
morning mist that obscured all but the blue-dawning sky,
Mahmoud Al Ramadi lowered himself to his knees facing the
sea. As he had still been afloat at the appointed hour of
devotion, he now offered Fajr ṣalāh, the dawn prayer. The
soothing ritual, while it lasted, obliterated the keening and
nattering from across the pebbly strand where he and dozens of
others had disembarked. He recited his two rak'ahs, adjusted
his cap, and slowly arose to survey the human specters
huddling nearby. Most of these ghosts, he assumed, were
displaced, dispossessed beings like himself seeking salvation
from grisly circumstances. He shared their aspirations for better
days abroad, but while almost all would make long, fraught

pilgrimages north, his odyssey would pause two hundred kilometers to the west, or so he hoped.

Through lifting fog he spied a Jeep and two white vans approaching along a two-lane road—security personnel or relief workers, he assumed. Having been cautioned not to get caught up in rescue operations, he took his leave, picking his way along the shoreline, avoiding migrants, cast-off life preservers, and the sorry flotsam of improvised exigency: Plastic bottles and bags. A shoe, a scarf, even a pair of eyeglasses. A man with no complexion, reposed on his side, half-submerged, someone he might even have seen before.

Mahmoud hauled him onto the beach by the armpits and squatted beside him, ear pressed to chest. No breath or heartbeat, only the racing of his own blood. He pumped on breastbone until no more water spat out, then clamped onto purple lips to breathe life back into the luckless middle-aged man, without success.

So close after traveling so far for so long. Such a shame.

The man's right hand still clutched the strap of an oblong bag. Mahmoud worked it from his fingers, dragged it away, and unzipped it. Inside were sneakers, clothing, packaged food, a Qur'an, a cell phone, and a half-soaked leather purse tied with a drawstring attached to a lanyard. A glance up and down the beach brought him to his feet with the purse stuffed inside his jacket.

"Your misfortune grieves me," he murmured to his mute benefactor before walking on. "May Allah be with you in paradise." His unfeigned remorse for robbing a corpse was soon tempered by the thought Allah has provided this not for me, but for his work.

At the berm of the beach he crossed the road and strode uphill, heading north. When he'd lost sight of the beach he stopped to examine the contents of the purloined purse. Besides a roll of worthless Syrian dinars, it held several small gold coins and pieces of gold and silver jewelry, some with precious stones. Mahmoud smiled and gave silent thanks for his ticket to Piraeus.

The road veered from the coast and wound through scattered houses and vineyards to a more barren landscape. Cresting a hill, he spied the harbor he'd noted from his overburdened Zodiac that sheltered several sailboats and fishing boats. Squinting revealed movement on one of them and he hastened downhill, stopping at a weathered store squatting behind two rust-pocked gas pumps. The slam of the screen door behind him roused the old woman at the counter to follow his rummaging with anxious eyes. Seizing a red plastic ten-liter gas can, he mimed to the matron his desire for some petrol, offering a fistful of dead-man dinars. She held one of the bills up to a dusty window, shrugged and wrinkling her nose tossed it back, muttering something he was glad he could not understand. Mahmoud scooped it up and in its stead presented a tarnished silver bracelet set with cerulean lapis. Her beady eyes glinted and her expression softened. She fingered the piece for a moment, tucked it in her tunic, and waved him out to take the fuel and be gone.

He topped off his canister with diesel and sloshed down to the limáni. On one boat a man was stretched out on a pile of fishing nets with his feet on the gunwales, chewing a cigar.

As he approached, Mahmoud fished out a gold ring with several small diamonds and another with what seemed to be an emerald, and slipped them on his left little finger. Displaying his multiple offerings, he hailed the boat's occupant, shouting "Athens! Piraeus!"

The fisherman had most likely been laying about that morning considering how he could profit from the frantic castaways down the coast, and now one had come to him. He struggled up and sniffed the contents of the gas can as Mahmoud ceremoniously offered up the rings. The mariner turned them in his leathery fingers, pocketed them, and with a sly smile again presented his palm. Aware he was at a disadvantage, Mahmoud reluctantly extracted a small gold coin from the purse, proffered it, and waved "enough."

His enticements worked. The captain motioned him aboard his vessel and cast off from the stone pier. Mahmoud followed him to the wheelhouse. As the wooden boat puttered past the jetty, the captain unrolled a coastal chart. Over his shoulder, Mahmoud located the port of Piraeus, traced a line to it, and received an affirmative nod.

The Aegean shimmered blue under a soft offshore breeze that barely ruffled its swells.

Mahmoud perched himself on the foredeck, back to the wales, grimly recalling how his commander had urged him to dispatch whomever ferried him and toss him overboard before entering port, lest he tell tales. But unwilling to betray the mariner who would shepherd him through strange waters, he decided the order was moot. Let the captain tell whom he will; no one would think twice about his helping a refugee move on.

Twenty minutes out to sea, a small ship looking like a coast guard vessel broke the horizon. Deciding he needed a hiding place, Mahmoud found he was sitting on one, a hatch cover. He shoved it away and jumped in to hunker in bilge in the company of rotting fish carcasses, nauseously rocking in the wake of the passing ship. When the sloshing stopped, he warily boosted himself up, replaced the cover, and lay on it. When he judged it was noon, he faced the stern and made two *rak'ahs* of *Zhur*, the noonday prayer. He recited prayers as often as he could. He didn't swear, smoke, or fornicate, and had rarely tasted alcohol. He had come to feel his prayers sometimes were heard. Considering all the perils he had recently negotiated, had he been a blasphemer he would have called himself damned lucky.

As daylight dimmed, Piraeus approached. The sturdy old boat puttered past high-rises perched on the shadowed cliffs of Piraiki in gathering dusk. Mahmoud gestured at a quiet cove, away from the busy harbor. His pilot obliged and nosed in as far as he dared. Before wading ashore, Mahmoud tipped him with a fifty-dollar bill for more fuel. There, on a patch of sand under an embankment, queasy, half-soaked, weak, he offered evening prayer and then reposed with his head propped on his backpack.

He had a right to be tired. His revolutionary path, which he had been assured would be righteous and glorious, now stretched across three thousand kilometers. As a reward for saving his life, his commander at the Eastern front had sent him off to Greece to be a key player in a special operation, disclosing nothing of its nature. Whatever that mission was to be, he knew it wouldn't animate the ashes of his parents in Mosul, and that was the point.

Some serious avenging needed to be done.

Most of what jihad had entailed so far he could have done without: His battalion's bitter retreat into Turkey after dodging ISIS bullets in Tal Aybah, then being put onto a lorry to lurch across Anatolia in the company of Kurds, whom he had to pretend were his saviors and was now glad to be rid of. At the edge of Asia Minor, having to trust his fate to seedy smugglers who relieved him of much of his money for the privilege of rafting to Chios, crammed against mothers anxiously stroking wailing children and furiously bailing fathers.

Having survived all these and other miracles, here he was in Europe. Feeling thankful, ill prepared and adamant, he clasped his hands behind his head and stared into the darkening sky, telling himself I can do, must do this which was meant to be. For Allah. For Iraq. For my parents and my brother. For liberation. For salvation.

His eyes soon closed and he slept fitfully until dawn. Vivid dreams, borne by disorientation and pangs of hunger, soothed his slumbering brain. He was in a small orchard on a verdant, sunlit mountain slope. Comely maidens were plucking apples from the trees, laughing and smiling as they filled their baskets with ripe, red fruit, their breasts gyrating their flowing gossamer robes. In the distance, atop a hill, a flag fluttered on a tall pole. "No virgins for you yet," a voice told him. "You must first climb that hill."

Yawping seabirds and grey glimmers of light extinguished his dream, leaving him with hunger, a headache, and a hard-on. He picked himself up and gazed up the rocky escarpment he would have to climb to reach the promised flag. But first, he knelt to the rising sun to offer Fajr ṣalāh, after which he relieved himself in the bay, stripped away his salt-stiffened clothes, donned khaki pants and a blue polo shirt from his backpack, and interred the foul garments he had worn for weeks under sand and rocks. He drained his canteen into his parched mouth, scrambled up the steep slope, and boosted himself onto asphalt. There, on an esplanade along the bay, he surveyed his surroundings, a row of tall, balcony-laden buildings. At the next corner he came upon a sidewalk café he would have entered were it not shuttered. Soon the street diverged from the bay into the shadows of apartment blocks. He trudged through the canyon hoping to be greeted by a place to eat and a public telephone.

His quest was rewarded at a large intersection with a small café, open for business.

Hunger drove him inside to gulp down a half-liter of water and tear into a square of spanakopita, bread, olives, tomatoes, and refreshing tea for an eagerly accepted ten-dollar bill.

Spreading his fingers into the universal phone gesture, he asked the proprietor "Telephone?" and was waved down a cross street.

A brisk five-minute walk brought him to a bus stop and close by, a pay phone. Hoping that it worked, he inserted his phone card and punched in his contact's number from memory, praying that he had gotten it right and that the call would go through without interception.

Anxiety swelled as the number started to ring. His contact's code name had slipped from his mind. He managed to retrieve it along with his own nom de guerre just as a gruff voice spoke in Turkish:

"Efendim!"

"George, is that you?" Mahmoud replied, also in Turkish.

"Who is this?"

"It's Peter," breathed Mahmoud. "I am here, praise Allah."

"I've been waiting, Peter. I have heard good things about you. We have much to do. Did you come alone, I hope?"

"Yes. I paid a man to take me here from Chios. A fisherman. Now what should I do?"

"Your host awaits you. Do you know where to find him?"

Mahmoud suppressed a snort. "Of course not. I don't even know where I am or what day this is."

George's voice lowered and hissed, "It's Saturday. No one gave you his address?"

"No. I would have remembered it," Mahmoud told him, adding "I thought you would board me."

"Not me. Where are you? Describe it."

"On a long street at a bus stop. It's spelled X-A-T-Z-H-K-something. Behind me is a wall around what looks like a campus or park. I see water way down the street."

"What direction are you walking?"

"Looks like the street goes north," Mahmoud said, noticing the morning sun at his right. "It's very straight."

George told him to hold on while he consulted his city map. Mahmoud stood nervously, his back turned to traffic, until George picked up and told him "I know where you are. It's called Marias Chatzikiriakou Street. Keep walking north. The street will end near some cruise terminals at a boulevard called Akti Miaouli. When you get there, go to the nearest bus stop and pretend you're waiting for a bus. Our comrade will meet you there and take you to his place."

"How will he know me?"

"Tell me what you are wearing."

Mahmoud described himself: 180 centimeters tall, ragged black beard, dark brown eyes, blue shirt, khaki trousers, grimy tan windbreaker, baseball cap, and a black backpack.

George said "Be there in half an hour and stay put. He is on his way. His name is Andreas and he will know you as Peter. Do not use your actual name, whatever it is. Nobody needs to know." George clicked off before Mahmoud could ask him what Andreas looked like.

Marias Chatzikiriakou Street sloped down before him, long and straight, ending at a patch of dark blue-green water. He started walking toward it at a brisk pace, chanting Andreas, Peter; Andreas, Peter.

Sooner than he'd expected, the street ended at the edge of a circular parking area overlooking several cruise terminals. Next to him was what looked like a church, with a cross atop a tower. No activity, only a scattering of city buses occupied the divided road that ran by it.

It should be easy for Andreas to see me here.

At the empty bus stop in front of the church he paced the sidewalk. Then, feeling too conspicuous, he retreated to the corner of the church to impatiently loiter. After about ten minutes, a police car came down Marias Chatzikiriakou and stopped at the intersection. Its driver eyeballed him from behind his shades before turning right and slouching down the boulevard. A few fidgety minutes later, a police car, possibly the same one, approached from that direction. It passed by, doubled back, and stopped in front of him. Mahmoud stood warily erect, his mouth suddenly dry as the driver got out and approached. Yes, it was the same cop.

He was used to having strangers—Kurds, Turks, Syrians, superiors—take his measure, but being profiled by the Greek police wasn't part of that repertoire. What can I do?

I can't speak Greek, and if he finds I have no identification, I'll be detained for sure.

Unwelcome visions of months in a filthy jail cell and deportation hearings flashed before his eyes as the officer said something in Greek. Instinctively, Mahmoud waved his hands in bewilderment. The cop gave him the once-over, followed by another indecipherable question or command. Mahmoud unconsciously clenched and unclenched his fingers, causing him to think

Maybe I can convince him I'm deaf. He started gesturing as if he were signing, voicing grunts and mumbles for effect. The cop seemed to get it, because he started speaking louder and more slowly.

Emanating frustration with Mahmoud's impromptu miming, the officer pointed to his backpack, gesturing for him to remove it. Out of options, Mahmoud shrugged and was about to obey the order when he heard a voice from his right calling, "Peter! Peter!" and turned to see a man running toward them up the sidewalk, blond ponytail flapping. The man sprinted up and hugged him as the officer looked on. With his hand firmly attached to Mahmoud's shoulder, he spoke in Greek to the officer, who now began questioning the stranger.

Could this be Andreas?

It seemed to Mahmoud much longer, but probably only a minute passed before the officer turned and went back to his car. "Andreas," Mahmoud hissed, "is that you?" His new friend nodded, and draping his arm around Mahmoud's shoulder, started piloting him along the boulevard. Soon he stopped, stepped back, and started to mime sign language at Mahmoud, whispering "Keep waggling your fingers!" Mahmoud complied and they pantomimed as the police car overtook them and sped away.

Honorable Mention

New Country

Laurence Jones – Surrey, United Kingdom

The road of excess leads to the palace of wisdom.

– William Blake, *The Marriage of Heaven and Hell*

BOOK ONE – Flagstaff, Arizona, Fall/Winter 1989

1. There's Been an Accident

Sheriff James Marston arrived at the scene just as they dragged the burned out wreckage of Jennifer Anderson's truck back up the mountainside. There had been a call on the radio then blue lights, paramedics, rain and flame. Jennifer's husband, Luke Anderson, had reported his wife missing a few hours before and Marston had promised his old friend one thing.

We'll find her, he said and he was right.

A charred figure lay crumpled and broken against the windscreen of the truck, a slender silhouette fused in to the dark structure of the dashboard like a sculpture.

Marston did not need to see anymore. He volunteered to break the news to her husband and left the scene as fast as he could.

He headed westwards, dwarfed beneath a dark sky bloated with angry storm clouds, his squad car headlights pushing bravely against the darkness of the desert road ahead. Marston fumbled for the pack of cigarettes on the dashboard, lit one, and waved the smoke from his face. He gripped the steering wheel tight and watched the cigarette burn against the darkness in front of him, duty bound and alone on an empty road. In the rear view mirror, a solemn reflection glanced back at him. His eyes were bloodshot and sunken in their sockets, his nose was still filled with the smell of scorched earth.

A sudden crackle from the radio made him jump.

We need you back just as soon as, said a woman's voice. It just keeps on flying back here.

Understood, said Marston.

There was a brief silence.

Are you okay? said the voice.

I'm fine, said Marston but, for a moment, he thought about turning back.

He peered out through the rain soaked windscreen and followed the road as it snaked downwards around the mountainside, his eyes focused on the metal barrier as it curved over the treetops. The inside of the car was filled with cigarette smoke and the static hum of the radio, but Marston barely noticed. All he could think about was Jennifer's truck, a mass of twisted metal and shattered glass. He drove carefully, preparing the words for the news he carried, trying not to think of the devastation it would cause and the ghost it would leave behind.

Eventually, the incline levelled out and the rain began to pelt loudly against the roof again. He arrived at a familiar crossroads, a set of traffic lights hanging high in front of him, their metal frame shaking precariously in the wind. The ground beneath him was bumpy as he left the tarmac of the interstate and headed out onto the desert road. It was the same route he had driven a hundred times or more but never had the Anderson ranch seemed so remote. Dark mountains loomed beyond it, their jagged peaks piercing the storm clouds and an unnatural grey light dripping through.

Marston parked close to the garage door, turned the ignition off then sat and stared at the house. There was a flash of light as the blinds in a downstairs window moved to one side then fell back in to place. Moments later, two towering spotlights exploded into life and lit up the Anderson estate, a working ranch converted to a family home, a temple to a dream that had passed.

Marston took his cigarettes from the dashboard, buried them deep in his coat pocket, and stepped out into the rain. He walked slowly across the mud and slush toward the house and let the cold rain soak him, unsure what he would say when he got there. He didn't want to arrive.

A figure appeared in the doorway. Lucky Luke Anderson was forty five years old and wearing blue jeans and a checked shirt. He looked at the police officer on his driveway and froze. Marston stepped onto the porch and swept the water from his jacket and hat.

Lucky, he said.

Lucky walked back into the house without a word and Marston followed. He closed the front door behind him, the wind and rain seeming suddenly distant, as if he had stepped into another world entirely. Lucky was sat on the stairs in the hallway.

He stood up and went to speak.

You might want to sit back down, said Marston. Lucky's face went white.

Luke. I got no right way to say this. There's been an accident. They been trying to call but we got cables down everywhere and all hell breaking loose.

He paused.

Where is she? said Lucky.

Marston steadied himself. She's been in a car crash, he said. She didn't make it. I'm sorry.

Lucky was quiet for a moment. How do you know? he said, his voice cracking.

Marston steadied himself for the executioner's strike. I was there, he said.

They found her truck and it was all burned up. They found her in it. She's gone, Luke.

The house felt colder all of a sudden.

She's gone, said Marston again.

Lucky stared at the floor then began to shake his head. Outside, something metallic grated and whined under the force of the wind.

I'm sorry, Lucky, said Marston.

Lucky stood up and launched his right fist hard against the wooden hallway panels, sending photos frames crashing to the timber floor below. He threw the same shot, again and again, until the panel was completely caved in. All the while, Marston simply stood and watched, no stranger to the language of devastation, until eventually Lucky turned to face him, his fist bleeding and covered in deep splinters. He went to speak then walked off instead, running his battered hand against the wall as his legs trembled beneath him. He vanished from sight into the kitchen. Marston waited. He knew the storm was not over.

There was a flash of silver and a sudden crash as a microwave hurtled across the kitchen and smashed into the fridge. Seconds later, Lucky followed it into view.

He picked it up again and hurled it against the wall above the stove. Still it was not enough. Stepping over the debris, he grasped one of the cupboards and ripped it from its fittings, condemning an avalanche of crockery to a broken grave at his feet. Lucky moved out of sight but the destruction continued, plastics and metals bouncing heavily against on stone floor, the percussive crash of pots and pans reverberating around the house. And so it went on.

In the hallway, Marston sat down on the stairs where Lucky had been. He picked up one of the photo frames from the floor. The glass had shattered inside the frame and the print below was faded and washed out with age. In the centre, Jennifer Anderson stared back at him from a hospital bed, surrounded by jagged shards, her long dark hair and cobalt blue eyes shining. She was holding her daughter Molly in her arms, only a few hours old, but somehow already blessed with her mother's spirit.

The pair of them were unmistakably the same flesh and blood. In the background, holding them both, his smiling face layered and scarred by the white cracks of fractured glass, stood Lucky Luke Anderson.

Marston propped the photo up against the wall, lit a cigarette and waited.

Young Adult Novel Excerpt

Finalist Judge – M.R. Street, Tallahassee, Florida

First Place

Darla Dreaming at the Carnival with Elvis

Carole Stice – Nashville, Tennessee

"Why do you even bother coming to school?" Marci said. "Nobody wants you there. Why don't you stay here where you belong, with your own kind?"

Still snickering, the girls disappeared down the stairs.

Darla unclenched her fists and rubbed her palms where her nails had dug into them. She didn't follow the girls. If she got into a fight it would only upset Dwayne. She hoped he hadn't heard what Gina called him. Darla still wanted to hit somebody, but carneys never start the fight; they just finish it.

When the final applause faded and the act ended, a man standing beside her said, "Damn they're good. I thought he was coming over the top edge for sure that last go-round."

"I don't know how they keep from getting killed," his friend said.

Had those guys never heard of centrifugal and centripetal forces? How could people think her parents would risk their lives for five buck a pop at the carnival? Nobody was that stupid.

When she was little, she had worried that her parents could get hurt or even killed doing their act until her daddy took her on the Round-up and showed her how those forces held her in place against the metal cage. "You can't hardly move your little finger can you?" he said. And she couldn't.

"As long as it flattens out and slows down gradually, you're as safe as if you were home in bed," he told her. "Riding our motorcycles is pretty much like that because of all the contraptions we have and because I know just how fast to go." So when he claimed what they did for a living wasn't really dangerous, she'd believed him. Now she knew the act was a little risky, but certainly not 'death-defying'—except in the case of a freak accident maybe. But that was true of lots of jobs. Besides, her folks wanted "rubes" to believe that the worst could happen any moment. That was good for business. And when it came to business, carneys never gave away trade secrets.

Darla had a love-hate relationship with the carnival. On the one hand, she like being part of the carney family, knowing all the tricks carneys use to rook folks out of their money. It meant she wasn't a "rube," wasn't a fool to be taken advantage of like they were. Living in town for more than three years now hadn't changed that. But the way some of the other girls treated her made her want to be anything but carney. Of course she'd never let them know that. When her teachers began telling her she was smart enough to do or be whatever she wanted, Darla was torn. Up to then, all her hopes and dreams had seemed totally out of reach. But last year she'd done really well on the ACT.

And all of a sudden it appeared she might actually have choices. She was no longer merely "that girl from the carnival." She could go somewhere else, be someone else.

But....

"There you two are. How you doing?" Mr. Carl Tharp, her daddy's general handyman and driver, was grinning from ear to ear.

"We're good," Darla said. "How 'bout yourself?"

"Doing great. How's your grandmother?" he asked, giving Darla a sideways hug and patting Dwayne on the shoulder. "I haven't seen her, or the two of you either, since before we left on the summer circuit." The summer circuit was the traveling part of the carnival. It started the first week in May playing gigs across the southeast, and ended the first of November.

"Grandma Diamond's okay," Darla said. "She just needs a break from having to take care of Dwayne and me all the time."

"Well, she is getting on up in years," Mr. Carl said.

"She's only sixty-nine," Darla said. "But she's got arthritis so she hurts a lot and it makes her cranky."

Mr. Carl nodded, rubbing his right shoulder. "I can understand that."

Mr. Carl had started working for Darla's daddy almost fifteen years ago—when Daddy was first thinking about going with the carnival, right after Mr. Carl had gotten out of prison for passing bad paper. From the first, Darla had liked him. Nights her parents stayed out all night, it had helped knowing Mr. Carl was asleep in the back of the big truck just a few yards away, if he was sober. Nights he wasn't sober, Darla stayed awake as long as she could, huddled by the trailer door, hoping one of her parents would come home soon. Drunk, Mr. Carl tended to wander around in circles arguing out loud with people who weren't there.

"I'm going to ride a motorcycle too when I grow up," Dwayne announced.

"What?" Darla started. Dwayne had never said any such thing before.

"Don't worry, Darla," he told her. "I'll only ride my motorcycle to school or the park and the Dairy Dip. Not inside the Vortex of Death. I promise."

Mr. Carl laughed. "You won't be needin' no motorcycle for a long time." He pulled Dwayne's baseball cap playfully down over his eyes. Dwayne took the cap off.

Darla peered down into the Vortex again. Daddy and Mama were putting their bikes in the storage room. "Hey Daddy," she called and waved.

Both parents looked up. Daddy grinned and waved back.

"Darla," Mama yelled. "Run down the Midway to Joe Clyde's joint and pick up supper. Hot dogs and fries for everybody. And don't forget extra ketchup."

Damn. Now she was going to have to buy supper and Mama wouldn't even offer to pay her back.

After saying goodnight to Mr. Carl, Darla shoved her long hair behind her ears and reached for Dwayne's hand. "We gotta go. We need to get supper and get you settled in," she said as she led him carefully down the steps.

"You get supper," Dwayne said. "It's almost time for my favorite movie."

At nearly twelve, Dwayne was too old for *One Hundred and One Dalmatians*, and he'd probably seen it fifty times already anyway. He needed new experiences, but he didn't much want them.

The Diamonds' old travel trailer and banged up truck that hauled the Vortex during the summer were parked away from most of the other carney tents and makeshift trailers. Daddy set up behind the Hootchie Kootchie tent, part of the permanent carnival at the Liberty County Fairgrounds, but still inside the chain link fence that surrounded everything. He did that so he and Mr. Carl could keep an eye on the Vortex.

Dwayne picked up a stick and dragged it back and forth along the fence making putter-plink sounds as they walked.

The trailer was still a good two hundred yards from the Vortex. Maybe if they walked slowly, Mama and Daddy would catch up and she'd get Daddy to pay for supper. Darla glanced back at the Vortex. The music was off and so were the lights, but there was still no sign of her folks.

Daddy, Mr. Carl, and Big Bill Lomax, Mama's old high school boyfriend, had built the enormous, two-story, wood and steel Vortex, plus all the rigging that went with the act. Freddie Schmidt, Carnival World's owner, had paid for it and dubbed it the Vortex of Death. Her daddy and Mr. Carl called it a Motordrome. Calling it a fancy name like Motordrome didn't make it any safer. On the other hand, like her daddy said, calling it the Vortex of Death didn't make it one bit more dangerous, either.

"Darla?" Dwayne said. "Why did that pretty girl call me a retard?"

Darla snapped to attention. She stopped walking, unsure what to tell him. In six months those girls and Darla would graduate from high school and Darla would be valedictorian or at least salutatorian, a situation that infuriated several students including those three. They were popular, but not particularly smart. Being smart and a carney tilted their tiny worlds just enough to drive them bat-shit crazy.

She sighed. "They're jealous because during the winter we get to go to the carnival whenever we want and they don't."

Dwayne seemed to consider the jealousy angle.

"That girl may be pretty outside," Darla added, "but inside she's just plain mean and ugly and after high school, no one much will ever like her again."

"You don't like her now," he said.

She put her arm around his shoulder. "No, I don't and that why she's mad at me. So she called you a name to hurt my feelings."

Dwayne frowned and appeared confused. He had been oxygen-deprived during birth so he was a little slow -- and then there was his deformed foot. Ever since he was born, Darla had helped look after him and home school him. Then when she started high school, she and Dwayne had moved to nearby Azure Lake, Florida to live with their grandmother on a tree-lined street in a house with a wide front porch and big backyard instead of living in their small travel trailer at Carnival World. Darla liked having a real house and Dwayne had improved a lot going to that school for special needs kids.

He smiled up at her. "It hurt your feelings 'cause you love me, right?"

"Absolutely. You got it," Darla said, glancing behind them again. "Oh good. Here come Mama and Daddy."

~~

2. The Grouch Pouch

Mama drank a beer outside sitting on a rickety green lawn chair with her feet propped up while Daddy walked down to Joe Clyde's to buy their supper. After Darla got Dwayne settled in front of the TV, she didn't have much unpacking to do. She refolded their clothes and laid them in two heavy cardboard boxes, which she shoved under the Futon in the trailer's tiny living room. By day, the Futon was their sofa. By night, it was where she and Dwayne would sleep. Once you took the scratchy brown cover off, it wasn't too bad.

The next day, around the crack of noon, Daddy and Dwayne went to the bathhouse to clean up. While they were gone, Darla took care of a little business. First, she carefully eased the Futon away from the wall, crawled behind it, and peeked out the trailer window. Mama was perched at the picnic table outside removing her stage makeup, which she should have done last night. Her portable radio blasted out Prince's latest hit, "Sign of the Times." Her hot rollers sat on the table beside her with an extension cord running all the way inside to the kitchen. Mama was going to curl her hair, which would take time.

Assured the coast was clear, Darla pulled a loose piece of paneling out from the wall and dug behind it for Dwayne's grouch bag and his precious cigar box. Tucked behind Dwayne's things was where she kept her own grouch bag. The loose panel was near the floor where no one was likely to find it since Mama never cleaned house anyway. Darla dumped the contents of her bag on the floor, a hairbrush, lipstick, earrings, and money. She counted. It was all there. Thirty-nine dollars and fifty cents, just the way she'd left it. She relaxed. With the four hundred fifty-two dollars and seventy-seven cents she pulled from her jeans pocket and deposited in the bag, she had nearly five hundred dollars cash. Mama might suspect she had nearly that much, but she'd think it was at Grandma Diamond's house in town. No self-respecting carney ever used an actual bank. That would involve taxes and a paper trail and the government.

At sixteen, Darla had gotten a part-time job at the Piggly Wiggly. Except for what she gave her grandmother for groceries and what she spent on Dwayne, she'd saved the rest. She hated having to quit such a good job when she and Dwayne had to move back out here to Carnival World for a couple of months. Hopefully they'd re-hire her after school started again in January. They'd said good workers like her were hard to find.

She snuck another look out the window. Mama had stopped rolling her hair half way through to smoke a cigarette. Darla hated that her parents smoked. Smoking was so stupid. No one would run into a burning building and go, "Wow, smoke. Great. Let me get a lungful of that."

She shook her head in dismay, hurriedly checked Dwayne's grouch bag and cigar box, then re-hid everything and quietly returned the Futon to its original position. She was determined not to let Mama find this hiding place or her savings would go the way most of her other money had—into her parent's poker, beer, and cigarette stash. Darla kept another grouch bag at her grandmother's house where it was probably safer, but like most carneys, she preferred to keep her cash-stash close by. Of course, the trailer, or even Grandma Diamond's house, might burn down, but since every carney kept a hidden money stash somewhere, they were all very careful about fire.

Money was her ticket out—if her teachers weren't just being nice to make up for girls like Gina. Darla had some idea what she wanted to do, but she had always pushed the notion out of her mind as ridiculously unattainable for a girl like her. Lately, however, she had begun to think maybe it wasn't just a wild dream after all.

Following lunch, while Dwayne watched cartoons and Mama got dressed, Darla decided to have a little daddy-daughter talk. Better to let him know now, get it out in the open rather than spring it on him later. Delbert Diamond was not fond of surprises.

He was outside at the picnic table smoking and cleaning his fingernails with a pocketknife. The sun would come out later and turn the day warm with clear skies, but for now the November air was chilly, with a sky the color of one of Mr. Carl's dingy undershirts. Darla wrapped her sweater around her, sat down beside her daddy. Without too much hemming and hawing, she launched into the speech she'd been rehearsing for weeks all about how she was good at school especially math and science and that she wanted to leave the carnival after graduation and do something different.

He listened, staring mostly at his fingernails or the ground while she talked. When she finished, he rubbed his stubbled chin. "After graduation you'll be free as a bird. Why not work for the carnival this summer?" He didn't look mad exactly, just puzzled. Darla stood up. The sand beneath her bare feet was still damp from the fast-moving thunderstorm that had blown through before dawn. She shivered.

"I want to try something else, that's all. I thought you ought to know."

He looked up at her with one eye closed. "Even if it means driving you and Dwayne the ten miles to school every single day between now and next May I'm glad to do it, because I swear Darla Kaye, living in town is giving you airs like you think you ain't real carney no more."

Her shoulders slumped. This was going to be harder than she thought.

Second Place

Water Cathedral

Kara Oakleaf – Burke, Virginia

Chapter One

Here is what she remembers:

Her boots slipping against the tree trunk as they pulled themselves up through the bare branches.

The way Maggie wove her scarf between her fingers and over her palms, because the branches were cold, and she'd lost her mittens last winter.

The tiny green and purple fibers Maggie's scarf left clinging to the bark, a trail of silk thread for Ellie to follow as she climbed up after her sister.

How the distance to the ground seemed to have shrunk since the last time they'd climbed up there, when they were much smaller. She remembers the thatched rooftops of their neighbors' houses, one street over. The forest had felt like a vast wilderness when they were younger, but she saw now the trees only covered a small patch of earth between the backyards of their street and another road less than a quarter mile away.

Their initials carved side by side with a hunting knife, the mark their father scratched into the tree to show how high they'd risen one summer. Years old now, it looked like an old scar on the sycamore's thick skin of bark, long healed and only a memory of the cut.

The little twigs at the ends of the branches, encased in ice and glinting in the sunlight.

Then, she remembers sitting there, legs dangling from the top and swinging back and forth; the feeling that the branch under her thighs might freeze to her jeans. The cold filling and stinging her lungs from the inside when Maggie told a joke and she couldn't stop laughing, drawing more of the cold in with each gasp to catch her breath. And finally, she remembers reaching out for something on a branch in front of her, something that looked like a single leaf frozen in place, her gloved hands gripping the branch and pulling herself up on it, and then the loud crack.

These are the scraps of memory Ellie kept for herself, flashes of normalcy from the last minutes of her life, when everything still might have been okay.

She remembers the sensation of falling, of wind hitting the back of her neck and rushing around her, but she does not remember the fear, the sudden shock of being unmoored in the air. She remembers the sound of the small branches breaking apart around her as she rushed downward, but she does not remember the pain of them scraping against her face, scratching up her skin and bringing small red droplets of blood to the surface of her cheeks before she reached the ground. And finally, she remembers the sound of the snapping branches close against her face, loud and echoing in her head. They sounded to her like wood cracking in a fireplace instead of branches breaking in the open air, in the cold and ice of November so far from anything warm.

In the Children's Eden, Ellie couldn't get those small details out of her mind. Maggie's make-shift mittens, rooftops through the trees, cold air in her lungs and the sound of firewood in a hearth. And then nothing.

She couldn't remember the last words her parents spoke to her, or what prompted her and Maggie to walk through the woods two days after an early winter storm and a cold snap that left their whole neighborhood frozen under a layer of ice. She couldn't even remember the last thing she and Maggie said before she gripped the branch that was clearly too weak to hold her weight, or if Maggie watched her fall. She tried to find these things in her memory, replayed those moments with the same pieces always missing. She didn't understand how she lost the last words between herself and her family, because what was the use of memory if it couldn't hold onto something so important?

Over and over, she closed her eyes and pictured the threads of Maggie's scarf, clinging to the bark of the sycamore, and waited for them to lead her somewhere.

In her first days, she filled the empty spaces of her memory with questions she could not answer. What did Maggie do, and would it change her forever, to have seen what she saw? Who told their parents, and were they angry that, even at fifteen, their daughter had been careless enough to hang from the branches of a frozen sycamore? What were they doing at this moment, and this moment, and the next moment without her? Ellie asked without being answered, the caseworkers always telling her some things are simply not meant to know.

Some things she might learn much later:

That her sister had scrambled down the tree and tried to wake her up, and that when Ellie didn't respond, her eyes opened and staring vacantly into the air, Maggie ran out of the woods to the nearest street and screamed until people came out of their houses, then rushed back indoors to call for help.

That it took several hours for her to die, her body kept alive by a respirator while a stranger in a starched white coat told her parents they could not detect any brain activity, and he was so sorry for their loss, and would they like to consider organ donation?

That her mother cried to the point of collapse and had to be carried to a hospital bed, but managed to collect herself long enough to sign the release forms, because her father had agreed to organ donation but couldn't take the final step that would allow the doctors to carve his child's body into pieces.

That her father did not cry for five days, but instead wandered around with a blank, pale look of shock on his face until after the funeral, and then he crawled into bed for two weeks. That Maggie finally laid next to him the way they had done as children waking from a nightmare, and begged him to get up, just for a little while.

That her school gathered all of the students in the gymnasium the following Monday to listen to the principal explain how one of their fellow students had died, though most of them, by then, had already heard the story.

That Will, her Will who had first kissed her in the dark of his parents' storm cellar, who mailed her postcards from every state in the west that summer and came back still wanting to kiss her, sat under the bleachers as the rest of the school bowed their heads and prayed for her, and that he did not come out of hiding until the end of the day.

About her friends. Caroline, who'd grown up alongside her, how she drifted silently through the school days with kids who she and Ellie would have called 'half-friends' descending on her between classes, jumping to be her lab partner or sit with her at lunch. All of them trying to help her feel less alone, but Caroline keeping silent and refusing to meet their gazes. How it would take another year before Caroline felt a part of anything. Simon, who spent hours backstage at the school theater with her, who like her had no interest in performing, but did the most perfectly detailed make-up, practicing on himself in the bright lights of the dressing room. How he used blue eyeshadow and lip liner to draw a tear below his eye every day for a month after she was gone. How one day, when a group of boys mocked him, Will overheard them and though he hadn't know Simon well at all, ran across the halls to defend him, shoving one of the other boys against a locker. He held him by the neck with both hands, shouting inches from his face, "just fucking let him be sad, okay? It's fucking sad," until two teachers pulled him off the boy and dragged them both to the office.

And years later, she might know about the people who lived, the ones sick or close to their own deaths on the day she died. The girl in the car accident who needed a transfusion, who would spend the rest of her long life with Ellie's blood running through her veins. The toddler, nearly blind, who saw his mother's face snap into focus for the first time with Ellie's corneas laid over his own eyes. The woman who received her kidneys and felt beautifully stunned to be alive each day for the rest of her life, and thought of Ellie as she watched her grandsons grow into teenagers. The teenager who'd lived years with a heart defect, whose name was Gabriel. He was the boy her parents would eventually meet, who would hug them and cry in front of them and let them touch his chest to feel a part of their daughter, still alive and pulsing like a melody through another body. The boy who wrote them letters from college and visited them and who they secretly sometimes thought of as their own son, one of the ways they got through the many years ahead of them without their second child. She learned about Maggie's daughter, named Eleanor after her own lost baby sister, and how Maggie realized too late that she couldn't call the baby 'Ellie' without becoming upset, and that was how the girl came to be known by her middle name.

In the Children's Eden, she learned her cause of death, listed in a tiny box on her hospital chart as internal bleeding and blunt trauma to the head, specifically the occipital lobe. She added new items to this part of the chart she'd formed in her mind, her own little box growing to accommodate all the reasons she was no longer in the world. Slippery boots, the way cold branches snap under weight instead of bending. Clumsiness, stupidity, thoughtlessness, the feeling of invincibility that every child seems to have until they don't.

She looked up the occipital lobe in an anatomy textbook in the library, and learned it is located at the back of the head, which meant she had been facing up before her eyes rolled into the back of her head and finally closed. The last thing she saw must have been the sky through the branches, or the sunlight caught in the icicle twigs, or Maggie, standing high above her. Ellie told herself it was Maggie, that the last thing she looked at in her life was her sister, but this wasn't part of her memory, and she would never know for sure.

~~

Chapter Two

Ellie Memory Files: Entry #7

Ellie's first memory, the furthest distance back into her childhood that she could recall, was also a memory of falling.

2018 Seven Hills Review

She lived in the same place all her life, a small Queen Anne in a small town in Ohio, which always felt to her like a small state. The house was nearly a century old by the time she was born. The staircase to the second floor had a rail on either side, one running along the wall and the other overlooking the hall on the first floor, carved wooden spindles like the bars of her crib supporting the rail. Ellie, at two, could not reach the railing, and when she climbed awkwardly up or down the stairs, she grabbed onto the wooden spindles for support, moving her hands from one to the next and holding on tight before she would let her little legs move to the next stair. Left foot, right knee, right foot. The dark sanded wood of each step smooth and slippery under her bare feet, her soles still baby soft. Navigating the slight grooves worn into the center of each step, the deep stain of the wood faded to the color of milk chocolate.

One day, she wakes from a nap and climbs out of her crib. On the stairs, she hears her father's voice calling to her. Her father has a big voice, a booming voice that seems to come from everywhere, and she looks around before she finds him standing in the hallway below her, waving both of his arms up at her. His waves are like his voice, large and with both arms.

"Did you wake up, Ellie-baby?" he asks her, and she laughs at this. She leans over to look at her father, one spindle in each hand, and then the one in her right hand breaks apart from the railing and falls away, and before she knows what has happened, Ellie slips through the open space. Her shins knock against the edge of the stair as she falls, and a splintered piece of the spindle is still grasped in her tiny fist, falling with her.

Ellie's father catches her easily; she is not hurt but when she feels the impact of her own little body in her father's arms, she screams and cries like every bone in her body has been crushed. Her father talks to her between her sobs, holding her tight against him. He says over and over, it's okay, I've got you... it's okay, I've got you. He presses her head to his chest, covers the side of her face with one big hand, and Ellie hears his heart racing, pounding fast and hard against the inside of his chest, speaking into her ear. His whole chest rises with each beat, and she knows, instinctively, that he is scared too. She realizes it in the confused, hazy way that children sometimes do, an understanding even before they've found the language for it. It surprises her that someone so much bigger than her could feel fear; it is strange to her, the idea that adults can also be scared, that people don't reach a certain age where everything in the world is understood and they have nothing to be frightened of.

But soon, her father's heart slows; the pounding fading to a soft, steady tap in her ear. Her cries quiet as she listens, and her father rocks her back and forth in his arms, which feel so large around her.

The last thing she remembers of this moment is feeling protected and safe again, a calm returning. The relief that her father wouldn't drop her, the way the stairs had. The feeling that she is safe in her own body, because something much bigger than herself is taking care of her.

~~

Chapter Three

There are hundreds of waiting rooms in the Children's Eden. In some rooms, the floor is covered with white sand and you can hear the distant sound of waves, though there is no ocean there. Others resemble a forest, with dirt and moss floors and wide tree trunks to weave through and a canopy of leaves above. In some rooms, a river rushes down the center, wide enough that the children who find themselves on the banks of the river cannot make out what's on the other side.

Many of the rooms are pure white, empty of all color and sound except for the colors and sounds the children bring with them. There are no gates rising through the clouds, though. No angels or saints or thrones with gods perched high above, watching. They don't want the children to get the wrong impression.

Each day, over twenty thousand newly dead children arrive. The ones who don't expect to be there stagger through their waiting rooms, bewildered and believing themselves to be dreaming. They take their shoes off and curl their toes in the sand, or wander the room looking for the ocean they hear without seeing. They dip a hand into the river or wander through the trees, looking for a way out or to find the way they came in.

Others know. They don't understand Eden any more than the children who believe themselves to be dreaming, but they realize they've passed the moment of their own deaths. They've waited for something like this place. They notice that they aren't in pain, or that their pangs of hunger or thirst are gone, or that they've just opened their eyes for the first time in weeks or months, and they know.

She came back to these places. During her free time in Eden, Ellie sometimes separated herself from the other children and wandered back to the waiting rooms. Sometimes they were empty, sometimes she saw children with their caseworkers in the rooms, but each day she came back, she looked for a room like hers: one where a child waited alone.

More often than not, she found one. She waved and smiled to them from across the rivers, sat with her bare feet dangling over the water until the child on the other side mimicked her movements. She sat with them under the shade of the trees, or on the beaches, tracing shapes in the sand with her fingers.

Only twice did she talk with the dead child waiting there – the other times, she found someone who did not speak English and could only sit with them, neither of them able to understand the other.

But at least then they weren't alone.

Whether they could understand her or not, she always said the same thing first.

"It's okay. Someone is here, waiting for you."

During her last days there, she came to the waiting rooms only once. One of the forest rooms, all shadows and bits of false sunlight spilling through the treetops. A boy a few years younger than her waited there, wandering in and out of the trees and through a small clearing.

He never saw her, and she never spoke. She hung back, because even though someone would come to get him, someone who was kind and patient and would promise to take care of him, she couldn't tell him that anything in this placed called Eden was okay. And she couldn't tell him to run. There was nowhere to go.

Third Place

Missing

Keith Manos – Willoughby, Ohio

Chapter 1

It was a match Crestwood High should have lost, so they did. A 5-0 egg, in fact, and the score could have been worse, but the Dalton High coach pulled his first-string centers and wings in the second period. They couldn't even score against Dalton's reserves in the third period.

They?

Not we?

Well, it used to be we.

But not now. The truth is even if I had played, we probably still would have lost since our guys skated like they were pushing the puck up a mountain. During the third period I watched Coach Mac grimace and turn away when Billy Murphy's pass wobbled weakly into the boards. Dalton's wing surged toward it, scooped it with his stick, and in a breakaway scored their last goal with a long, twisting wrist shot.

Schmidt should have hip checked the kid when he passed the blue line. It wasn't all Billy's fault.

When his teammates mobbed the kid, the urge to be on the ice washed over me again. I saw last year, my junior year, the play-offs at the Eastgate Arena, and the crisp sparkle of fluorescent lights on the white ice. In my head, I heard again the scraping of my own skates and I felt the chill of the ice. The Crestwood crowd was in a frenzy, stomping on the bleachers, screaming as we set up the power play, the score tied 1-1 against Ridgebury, the black puck gliding and tapping easily along in front of my stick, the goalie, a flopper, squatting and shifting left and right in front of me, and finally my short side slap shot, a howitzer from my wheelhouse, which ended with solid thud into the net, sending our fans into one giant roar. Strangely, I even felt the heavy nylon of my blue and gold Crestwood High School jersey, prompting me to touch my jacket just to make sure I wasn't wearing it.

That was last season, this season's over. Let it go.

I told myself that I came to the Dalton match to show, of course, my support for the Cougars – c'mon, some of those guys were my friends –.

Not all true. You wanted to be out there, you wanted the puck, you wanted to crash the boards one more time.

I looked around. Few people came today to cheer the Crestwood hockey team, but those that did would turn in their seats and glance at me every now and then, their faces full of disappointment:

Why aren't you out there, kid? They need you. How could you just quit like that?

Refusing to let them make me feel guilty, I glared at them until they turned back to the action on the ice. Maybe I would have made a difference this season, maybe not, but why speculate? The season was over.

In my Before He Left life I was number 12.

Now, however, a freshman wore that jersey, and after both Crestwood and Dalton had cleared the ice, I sat there, staring at the vacant seats and empty rink. The only sound now was the relentless whine of the Zamboni, and the chill came from the giant fans used to refrigerate the place. As I said, Crestwood losing didn't really matter anyway. It was March, the match against Dalton was Crestwood's last, and I didn't wear the blue and gold anymore.

I didn't quit; he made me quit.

I attended the game alone, and, back in my car, I watched snow turn to slush as it hit the gravel of the Dalton's ice rink's parking lot. The clouds in the murky sky looked like the ugly columns of gray smoke that rose from Chicago's factories, their smokestacks just several miles away sticking up like dirty pillars. It figured that crummy weather came with losing.

I texted Marta.

They lost.

I turned the ignition, cranked up the heat, and waited only one minute before she responded:

Sorry. You ok?

Yeah. It was an easy lie. Easier to tell Marta that seeing Crestwood lose was no big deal. I had seen them lose other games this season, of course, and I had endured the stares of the fans in those games too.

Like it was my fault Crestwood sucked now.

The parents and fans didn't know the whole story; they only knew what they read in the newspapers or what they shared as gossip. None of them even asked me.

The snow continued to fall, the Buick's engine purred, and I drove out of the parking lot. When I turned on the radio, the seven o'clock Chicago Blackhawks game was just starting. They had been Dad's favorite team. Mine too. The Blackhawks were another Before He Left part of my life, so I turned off the radio. Silence was better than listening to their game against the New York Islanders and then remembering other games, especially the playoff run in 2015 when they won the Stanley Cup.

Get rid of thoughts like that. Think of things warm and wonderful.

A school counselor had told me to do that in a conference in her office last spring after several teachers complained about me being moody and missing assignments. "You control your reactions, Brian," she had explained, tapping a pencil on her desk. "An event can't make you unhappy. Only you can make you unhappy."

I made me unhappy? Really? I did that?

The counselor knew nothing about me; I'd been skating for ten years – Midgets, Juniors, high school.

All of it now for nothing.

Anyway, I decided to make myself feel better; that's why I drove to Crestwood High. I didn't want to go home or see my former teammates at a fast food place or drive around suburban Crestwood moping about a lost hockey season. Marta needed to know what I had decided to do. Actually, what I wasn't going to do. And I knew Marta was at the school, finishing the March issue of the Crestwood High School Chronicle.

This was my first year on the staff of the Chronicle. The advisor, Mr. Angelo, had asked me to sign up my senior year after I submitted a statistical piece about road kills on Illinois highways called "Road Kill: The Final Destination." He loved it so much he even gave me my own column. I called it "Only in

Crestwood" by Brian Cord. I for sure needed something else now to put on my college applications.

Marta, also a senior, was the student editor-in-chief and in charge of the front-page articles. "The big news," she had told me as she showed me the sections of an old issue trying, I think, to impress me on my first day on the staff.

Marta, I have to tell you, is cute. Real cute. Blue-green eyes, sandy-colored hair that barely touches her shoulders, white teeth, and at five foot nine she is three inches shorter than me. Signing up for the newspaper class, I decided, was a smart move.

Our first meeting took place in the Chronicle staff room where I grabbed another copy off a nearby table and looked at the front page. "New boilers installed," I read out loud. "Counselors announce ACT scores. Salad bar for cafeteria. Is this what they call investigative journalism?"

I was only kidding, but Marta grabbed the paper from my hands and waved it like a sword in front of my face.

"They're better than that thing you wrote about dead raccoons bleeding on Route 44."

"Jealous?" I asked with exaggerated concern.

"Disgusted," she answered sternly and went back to the layout table. Like I said, that was my first meeting with Marta Moyers, and after that I couldn't stop thinking about her.

I was glad when I saw her car in the school's parking lot and the lights on in the Chronicle staff room. Our next issue was due in three days, which meant extra hours for the editors. The Chronicle staff room was located in the school's basement, and the radio in the corner was playing Beatles music, Marta's favorite. Mr. Angelo and two other kids were leaning over a table at the other end of the room, scanning photographs.

"Hey," I said.

Marta swiveled in her chair in front of her computer, and when she gave me a quick look with her eyebrows arched, her eyes looked more green now than blue. "I figured you'd come here." And then: "Are you sure you're okay?" Her shoulders slumped a bit; she knew how much I still wanted to be on the ice.

Okay? I could have asked her to define the word. Was it okay Crestwood got shut out in the last game of the season? That no one could score, not even against Dalton's second team? Was it okay the way those parents looked at me?

"Yeah, I'm okay," I said flatly and pretended to be interested in the Chronicle's March edition. "What are you working on?"

"College plans for . . .." Marta's eyes widened. "Wait a minute, Brian. I almost forgot." Then she swiveled toward her computer screen and clicked on a new website. "I did some more research. I'm thinking now he's in California." She nodded at the screen.

"Almost forty million people live there; it's our most populated state. He could easily get lost there." She faced me again and smiled broadly.

I groaned. "A month ago, you thought he was in Alaska."

Marta frowned. "True, but that was because it's, you know, so up there . . . and so cold. Who would ever look for him there?" She shrugged and turned back to her computer. "I bet it's California."

"Marta . . ." But I stopped myself to recalculate how to inform her I had changed my mind. I hopped onto a nearby table and looked at her back and straight hair swaying left and right on her shoulders as she followed her words on the screen. I listened to Marta clicking on the keyboard and remembered our second meeting in the newsroom.

"Do you really want us to print this?" she had asked, peering at the computer screen and reading my second article titled "Is it just a Date or is it Fate?"

"Sure do."

"'You go to pick her up,'" she had read out loud, squinting at the screen and cringing after each paragraph, like she expected the words to leap off the page and strike her in the face, "'and you have to follow the traditional first date guidelines (details, mind you, I've gotten from reliable sources): (1) Meet the Dad, except he has always just finished a spaghetti or bratwurst dinner or something like that and he's belching all over the place. (2) Play with the dog, which typically tries to get friendly with your leg. (3) Compliment the Mom on her taste in curtains, even though plaid went out of style in 1970' . . . Mr. Angelo okayed this?"

"He thinks it's funny."

Marta stormed away, and another week passed before she would talk to me again.

I think she thought I was obnoxious. But after I texted her a line from a Beatles song, *I want to hold your hand* (corny, I know, but she is a huge Beatles fan), she finally agreed to go with me to Dairy Queen after school for one hour, as long as her girlfriend Jenni Phillips could go along.

I accepted her conditions right away. Jenni was okay, a senior like us, but she wore so much makeup she looked like a mannequin. I thought she'd order waxed fruit to eat.

After that, it was a movie – Johnny Depp as Jack Sparrow and Jenni Phillips munching popcorn. Next was the last home football game (without Jenni) and a day later, dinner with her family where they had chicken and corn on the cob. Her dad didn't burp once, and they had a cat, not a dog.

From then on we saw each other as much as possible. She showed me her paintings, and I taught her how to skate. She baked me chocolate chip cookies, and I ate every one of them.

Like I said, I couldn't stop thinking about her. That's because – and I'm kind of embarrassed to say this – she was the first girl I ever kissed. Before Marta, I guess I focused only on school and hockey – I needed the grades and the stats if I wanted to play in college.

I'd like to say it happened spontaneously. The kiss, that is. But it didn't. I planned it. Like a good reporter, I arranged the event according to the five W's.

WHO: Marta Moyers

WHAT: A real, honest, passionate kiss on the lips, possibly inserting the tongue, if accessible.

WHERE: The hiking trail in the park.

WHEN: Thursday, between 20-25 minutes after arrival.

WHY: Her lips look so soft, and I'm seventeen, and if I don't kiss someone other than my mother's crazy sister, who's always grabbing my face and squeezing my cheeks into pancakes, I will run naked through the halls at Crestwood High School.

We had driven after school in my mom's Buick to the park on one of those warm November days. "Someone's dumping toxic waste," I had informed her, "so bring your camera." That hooked her since she was always on a save-the-whales or save-the-trees or save-the-butterflies campaign.

She slung her camera over her other shoulder, the straps angling over her breasts, and allowed me to hold her hand, the Beatles song becoming a reality. We sauntered along, studying the foliage left and right, until we came to the spot I had marked out the day before. "Here it is," I said. She raised the camera and checked the flash.

"Where?"

"There," I pointed.

Marta lifted her camera, and then paused. "It's just a grocery bag, Brian." She lowered the camera, walked over to the bag, and nudged it with her foot, allowing a half-eaten sandwich and a crumpled bag of potato chips to spill out, flies buzzing around them. "Toxic waste?" She glared at me. "Where's this dumping ground you talked about?" She peered into the forest. "If you're lying to me, Brian, it's not funny. I've got econ' to study, you know. We have a massive test tomorrow."

"What did you expect? An oil slick?" I inched toward her.

"Certainly not this." She looked again at the damp bag.

"Then how about this?" I gently put my hands on her elbows, more to stop her from moving away than for any romantic reason, and pulled her toward my chest. Then I kissed her.

Her warm lips cushioned mine, and her hands moved to my shoulders to steady us. I was afraid to move an inch.

Breathe, I remembered. Breathe and go again. My mind fluttered with questions as my lips still pulsed, recalling the soft feel of hers against them. Should I move my tongue forward or back? Should I move my head around? Should I hug her more tightly?

We kissed again. I swallowed her exhales, stroked her arms, and felt her hands tug at my elbows.

Seconds later, Marta stepped back and opened her eyes. "You tricked me, Brian Cord." She smiled.

"Sorry." I grinned back at her.

"I'm not." She tilted her head towards mine, and we kissed again. Her hands held my face. When she pulled away, she said, "It was about time."

We walked back to the car, holding hands a little more tightly this time, and she even put her head on my shoulder. I felt like a king. I don't think I had to tell her I was falling in love with her.

Today, however, I wanted to tell Marta I was ending this search for my father.

You see, Marta got me into this Hunt for Arthur Cord investigation. Any real urge I had to find my dad had been squashed months ago, but after she learned my father had disappeared, Marta Moyers, the front-page editor, refused to let it go.

PENUMBRA POETRY & HAIKU COMPETITION

Poetry

Finalist Judge – Josephine Yu, Tallahassee, Florida

First Place

Leave Taking

Brad Barkley – Frostburg, Maryland

Funny, what you notice—the way the gasoline spill

In the driveway seems beautiful, a plate of shades,

And your brain wants to say something about finding

The exquisite in what's ugly, or the harmful

In what's pretty, and then you stop that. Just stop.

Enough. The ideas about the spill have no need

To be bigger than the spill itself, and so you find

A t-shirt, the one you bought in Ocean City in 1998,

And you call it an attractive accident, and you mop it up.

Or the way a board, half-rotted and hanging

From the eaves, the one you meant to nail back up,

Looks romantic in the way of tobacco barns, in the way

Of all dilapidation, and your brain, supple these days,

Wonders why it is that dilapidation is attractive

In buildings but not people, but then that's wrong too—

Consider the poor, washing their clothes in rivers,

Or photos of sturdy mountain people in church.

As long as it's not your building, not your person.

At night, your bones crack, while light from the clock

Reddens your shoes, your eyes feel wet and scalded,

While your brain, that old reptilian friend, watches

The ceiling fan cut the headlights into sticks.

Everything competes to be appealing and sad,

The night, so dark and menacing, is only

A sixth-grade bully, giving in without a fight.

How strange you note, in love anew with irony—

It is only with dawn that the crickets begin their requiem.

Second Place

Stillness

Teri Foltz – Ft. Thomas, Kentucky

I wonder how many
of William Henry Harrison's
32 days of Presidency
Were eaten up by sitting for that portrait,
Posing stone still while Congress passed
Laws he would have vetoed
Had Albert Hoit not spent such an inordinate amount
of time on his sharp edged nose.
There he sat regretting the long inaugural address
he gave in the cold rain
While he was forced to suppress the cough
climbing from his lungs.

"Please, Mr. President, stillness."

What thoughts must have played in his aging mind
while he sat crippled by Hoit's brush.
It's a good thing that cameras came before the next war so
That while the Confederate army was bombarding Fort Sumter
Lincoln did not have to sit in time out
Waiting for the artist to hollow his cheeks just right.

Third Place

The History of Everything

Eliza Callard – Philadelphia, Pennsylvania

I. Geology

Slices of slate one-inch thick

　　lean like playing cards as tall as me.

Drops of white lichen spatter striations.

A thousand million flecks of mica glint from Wissahickon schist,

　　from creek beds, bridges, and walls.

We scrabble over boulders any real climber would scorn.

II. Biology

And mosses: dry and pale, springy and inviting,

　　flowing underwater like the hair of Naiads

　　heading upstream on a protest march.

Robins hunt, and my grandmother sent me a Christmas card

　　with an English robin. Round and petite,

　　she said. "American robins are terribly gaudy."

III. Physics

The water tumbles and smacks over the weir.

　　Twist away and above: the woods are silent.

IV. Psychology

"We are the only ones who have ever been here," I say, despite

    dog tracks, footprints, real live trail runners

      in white and yellow spandex, this tree that has met an

      axe.

V. History

Indians used this forest before it was cut down and the mills

    bloomed and the mills left and the forest was replanted.

    Chief Tedyuscung, cut in stone, scouts the land.

Next to the gravel path, there stand

    benches and cabins created by men of the WPA,

    men saved by our sudden need to sit. The rough

    wood blends in like the faceless in soup lines.

    Hewn from the useless, their makework is beauty.

VI. Theology

On Sundays, my family hiked these city woods.

    My brother and I used the Sabbath to track deer, swing
      on vines,

    stalk each other.

VII. Anatomy

I pass a woman who smiles, half-knows me. Two decades ago,

    I sat for her girls. One screamed for her mother and
      writhed

in my arms. Her sister demanded again and again
   an instructional book

("Mom and Dad's Special Hug"), with a hairy
   cartoon couple baring it all.

VIII. Pathology

A pool of water under a bridge invites me to drink. There's
   sewage in these waters, says my

wife. "But it *looks* clean," I say.

   I feel strong here. I pant, I wheeze, I cough, but I
   walk.

IX. Anthropology

The curve of my wife's jeans ahead sustains me until we
   join the main path.

Sprawling mansions pull us up to the road. A sticker on a
   stop sign

      announces a concert by G. Love & Special Sauce. A
      croissant,

      a coffee, art on the walls, newsprint.

The history of food, joy, home, arrogance, humiliation,
   color, silence.

The history of everything.

Haiku

Finalist Judge – Katya Taylor, Tallahassee, Florida

First Place – "Mother's Day"

Ross Plovnick – St. Louis Park, Minnesota

Mother's Day
the forget-me-nots in bloom
by her grave

Second Place

Dream of My Lover

Eileen P. Kennedy – Amherst, Massachusetts

You hold me wading

the river rushing below

I cradle your shoes

Third Place

Sharpening

Ross Plovnick – St. Louis Park, Minnesota

sharpening

Dad's old camp knife

mountain air

Winning Author Biographies

Brad Barkley

Brad Barkley is the author of the novel *Money, Love*, which was a Barnes and Noble "Discover Great New Writers" selection and one of the best books of 2000 as named by the Washington Post. His novel *Alison's Automotive Repair Manual* was a "BookSense 76" selection. He has published two collections of short stories, *Circle View* and *Another Perfect Catastrophe*, and three YA novels. His short fiction has appeared in over thirty magazines, including *Southern Review, Georgia Review, the Oxford American, Glimmer Train*, and the *Virginia Quarterly Review*, which twice awarded him the Emily Balch Prize for Best Fiction. His work was anthologized in *New Stories from the South: The Year's Best, 2002*. Brad has won four Individual Artist Awards from the Maryland State Arts Council and a Creative Writing Fellowship from the National Endowment for the Arts. He lives in the mountains of Maryland with his wife Kristin and their dog Mille, and he enjoys flying hang gliders and playing guitar.

Jan Baross

Jan Baross began her career as a painter. That led to award-winning animation and documentary films. She taught filmmaking at Oregon State University and was a film critic as well as a journalist, cartoonist, screenwriter and playwright. Her debut novel, "Jose Builds a Woman," won first place for fiction in the Kay Snow Awards. Baross's MPOLO Press has published her three illustrated travel guides. Her second novel, "Redneck Central," is in process. Ms. Baross says, "I like to expand the adventure in as many directions as possible." She lives in

Portland, Oregon, and spends four months every winter in Mexico. Contact her at BMI@easystreet.net or visit her website, janbaross.com.

Carol Bullman

Carol Bullman lives in Texas with her husband and their two sons. She is the author of The Christmas House (Ideals Children's Books). When writing stories and poems for children, she becomes more of who she already knows she is. You can find her blog at www.achildrensbookworld.com.

Suzanne Burns

Suzanne Burns lives and works in central Oregon. She writes both poetry and fiction with an occasional dabble in personal essays. When she isn't writing she is hotly discussing the narrative arc of various Real Housewives series with her mom or researching vintage baking recipes to enter in the county fair each summer. She loves horror movies but always sleeps with a nightlight. She's never babysat once in her life.

Eliza Callard

Eliza Callard was born, raised, and now lives in Philadelphia with her family. Forty-odd years of managing -- and occasionally mismanaging -- her cystic fibrosis have given her an unusual perspective on loss and endurance. She likes to think she embodies some of the qualities of her city by being scrappy and friendly, and older than you'd think. (She also knows how to collapse her city's five-syllable name into the local two: 'Fluff ya'--which also, conveniently, sounds like an insult Rocky might throw). She enjoys family time, drawing, hiking, running, biking, swimming, and camping. She's been widely published, and her website is elizacallard.com.

Alice Cappa

As a fiber artist and writer, Alice enjoys mixing media and words, such as word collages with illustrations on hand-made paper and book-making with her stories. A few of her tales have been printed onto long scrolls of handmade papers. One was chosen by WFSU's former "Stories In The Air". *The Coat of Many Faces* is from that enchanted land. Alice has degrees in Art Education and Graphic Design and Multi-media. More information is at http://www.alicecappa.com/Wri/index-SH.html.

Katie Clark

Writer, poet, photographer, educator, all around dreamer extraordinaire, Katie Clark is from the Panama City Beach, FL. She gets inspiration for creative works from the beauty of North Florida. She received her B.S. in Education from Florida State University, PC, and is currently in the Instructional Systems Learning Technologies masters program.

Geoffrey Dutton

Geoff Dutton reads and writes whatever suits his fancy, mainly nonfiction, calling himself "a reality-based author." After an early career as a geospatial software engineer in academia and industry, Geoff spent the prime of his life as an IT columnist and a technical writer. He found time along the way to author hundreds of stories, nonfiction articles, memoirs, broadsides, and the odd poem, samples of which can be found at his site, progressivepilgrim.review. *Mahmoud's Jihad* is his first completed reality-based novel. Geoff lives in the Boston area, where he likes to forage for wild mushrooms and cook for his family (all are perfectly well, thank you).

Lyla Ellzey

Lyla Faircloth Ellzey lives with her husband in a retirement village in Tallahassee, Florida, where she volunteers for several committees to better serve the residents. Her passions are writing, reading, artistic attempts, and viewing art in the world's greatest art museums. Showing what the artist may have been thinking when painting a masterpiece, or giving the characters life and a story, is the stuff novels are made of. One such was Lyla's short story, "The Ewer Maiden," which appears in an earlier 7 Hills Review, and is based upon Matthis Stomer's painting of Jesus before Pilate, which hangs in the Louvre. She plans to write more about special paintings and the stories they tell.

Teri Foltz

Teri Foltz is from Ft. Thomas, Kentucky.

Kara Imle

Kara Imle hails from Kenai, Alaska. She started writing as soon as she could pick up a pencil. Her first stories were about a girl who loved wolves so much she decided to be one. Kara is currently finishing a memoir about growing up in Alaska, and the lines between reality and religion, imagination and madness. *Dangerous* is an excerpt from the rough draft. Kara's degree in creative writing led to a grant-writing assignment in West Africa soon after graduation. She is the ghost-writer of a book published in 2004. She appears in print and online publications including Crosscurrents Journal, the Desert Review, the Peninsula Clarion, Elephant Journal and her blog. Kara currently makes her home in Austin, Texas.

Laurence Jones

Laurence Jones was born and raised in London. His writing career began while studying American History, Literature, and Creative Writing at Northern Arizona University in the United States. His short stories have been published in COLLAGES (CCWC, 2013), an anthology of new writing, and NEW ZENITH MAGAZINE (November 2016). He also won the Conville & Walsh Discovery Day event in 2013, was a finalist in The Literary Consultancy's Pen Factor 2015 competition, and was long-listed for the LitRejections Short Story Prize in 2016.

Eileen P. Kennedy

Eileen P. Kennedy was nominated for a Pushcart for Banshees (Flutter Press, 2015) and was awarded Second Place in the Wordwrite Poetry Book Awards. She won Second Place in the Penumbra Poetry Contest and was awarded Honorable Mention by the New England, New York and London Book Festivals as well as the Tom Howard/ Margaret Reid Poetry Prize and The Oregon Poetry Society. She has published poetry In more than 25 literary journals and holds a doctorate in language and literacy.

John Koelsch

John was an Infantry Combat Platoon Leader with the First Division in Vietnam. In May 1968 he led his men against the heart of the Second Tet Offensive, preventing the VC from attacking Saigon. He continued to lead them into the August

3rd Offensive. He received a Bronze Star w. "V" Device for Valor, a Purple Heart w. Oak Leaf Cluster, and a Combat Infantryman's Badge. His Vietnam novel, *Cease Fire,* is in its final review before submitting for publication. John holds a B.A. in Political Science and a M.P.A. He received the 2015 Stephen J. Meringoff Writing Award in Non Fiction from the Association of Literary Scholars, Critics, and Writers for a chapter excerpt of *Cease Fire.* Between 2009 and 2017, John has won several awards from the National Veterans Creative Arts Festival Competition, including 13 Gold Medals, 12 Silver Medals, and six Bronze Medals. He is currently writing a book that contains the only peaceful solution to righting our government and saving our nation.

Keith Manos

Keith Manos is a veteran English teacher who was named Ohio's English Teacher of the Year (2000) by OCTELA. He was inducted into the National Honor Roll of Outstanding American Teachers in 2006. He is the author of nine nonfiction books, including *Writing Smarter* (Prentice Hall, 1998). Recently, Black Rose Writing published his debut novel, *My Last Year of Life (in School).* His articles and fiction have appeared in national magazines including *Wesleyan Advocate, School Library Journal, Teacher Magazine, Lutheran Journal, Visions, Wrestling USA*, and *Accent.* You can check out all his books at www.keithmanos.com.

Peggy McCarthy

Peggy McCarthy lives, works and writes in rural northern Indiana. After serving as an on-campus writing consultant for several years, she formed and facilitates a writing group. Whitley County Writers has offered encouragement, support, and seriously helpful critique for nearly fifteen years. McCarthy's work has been recognized for clarity, story-telling ability, and engaging characters.

Kara Oakleaf

Kara Oakleaf's work has appeared in journals including SmokeLong Quarterly, Monkeybicycle, Jellyfish Review, Nimrod, Tahoma Literary Review, and Postcard Poems and Prose. She is a graduate of the M.F.A. program at George Mason University, where she now teaches and directs the Fall for the Book literary festival.

David Oates

David Oates writes about nature and urban life from Portland, Oregon. He is author of four books of nonfiction, including "Paradise Wild: Reimagining American Nature." Recent essays have won first-place nonfiction awards (Northern Colorado Writers; Tiferet) and received Pushcart Prize nominations. He was a finalist for the Ironwood Trifecta in prose (2017). His prose and poetry are currently being featured in the German literary journal Wortschau, in German and English.

Tom Pelham

Tom Pelham is a retired lawyer, planner, and teacher who has written extensively about Florida's environmental and land use planning laws. He received law degrees from Florida State University and Harvard University and served as head of the state land planning agency under two governors. Tom grew up on a family farm in the rural Florida panhandle in the 1940s, 1950s, and early 1960s. He lives in Tallahassee, Florida, with his wife Vivian and is writing a memoir about his childhood years on the family farm.

Ross Plovnick

Ross Plovnick lives in St. Louis Park, Minnesota. He is a member of the Loft Literary Center in Minneapolis. Happily retired, he enjoys the outdoors in all seasons and the freedom to travel and explore the world with his wife. His poems have appeared in a variety of print and online journals, and in anthologies including *Seasons* (Poems from the Southwest Journal Poetry Project, Trolley Car Press, 2010), *Haiku 2014*, *Haiku 2016*, and *galaxy of dust: The Red Moon Anthology of English-Language Haiku 2015*.

Carole Stice

Carole Stice is a retired college teacher. Her work for children has appeared in *Highlights for Children* and *Ladybug*. She has a short story in the literary journal *Kestrel* and is also the author of two textbooks as well as articles in various academic journals and instructional materials. Her most recent effort, *Always Yours: Memoir of an Adopted Child*, is available from Amazon books. In addition to writing, she enjoys traveling and playing bridge. She lives with her husband and two cats in Nashville, Tennessee.

Sydney Watson

Sydney Watson is an author, adventurer, Florida native, and English professor who has published articles about Old Florida and written for scholarly journals. Her novel, Island Salt, awarded Best Book Finalist by USA Book News was set in the Bahamas where Sydney lived with her husband for eight years. Sydney continues to write creative nonfiction and fiction and has won numerous awards. She has lived on the Forgotten Coast of Florida with her husband and three Labradors for the past three years, loving the solitude of the region.

2017 Finalist Judges

Randi Atwood – Creative Non-Fiction

Randi Atwood started her career as a professional stage manager and theater director. She toured until she could no longer do without the finer things in life, like an apartment and health insurance. For nearly 15 years she was the associate director of the Council on Culture & Arts (COCA), and joined the Tallahassee Democrat as entertainment editor in 2012. She is now the platform editor, a job title no one understands, and teaches nonfiction writing and theater at the Osher Lifelong Learning Institute in Tallahassee.

Jenny Jeffers – Short Story

Jenny Jeffers professional life as a data and internet security guru would surprise many who know her as the enthusiastic owner of My Favorite Books, a local new and used bookstore in Tallahassee. Her love of books, and authors has brought her into the Tallahassee Writers circle of friends for her unfailing support of local talent in the North Florida region.

Rob MacGregor – Adult Novel Excerpt

Rob planned to study archaeology, but ended up majoring in journalism. Over the next dozen years, he worked as a reporter and editor, but never gave up his interest in ancient civilizations. Between jobs and on vacations he explored archaeological sites in Mexico, Central and South America, Europe and North Africa. Those experiences came in handy when he wrote six original Indiana Jones novels for LucasFilm and Bantam Books. After finishing his seventh Indy novel, he studied shamanism through the Four Winds Society. As a result, more magic happened and he wrote a young adult Native America mystery series, including *Prophecy Rock*, which won the Edgar Allan Poe award for mystery writing in 1996, and *Hawk Moon*, which was a finalist for the same award the following year. He's published 20 novels and 18 non-fiction books, and collaborated with George Lucas, Peter Benchley, and Billy Dee Williams. *Seven Hills* is honored to have Rob's insights on our Adult Novel Excerpts.

M.R. Street – Young Adult Novel Excerpt

M.R. Street is an award-winning author of middle-grade and young-adult fiction. Her novels include *Blue Rock Rescue*, *The Werewolf's Daughter,*and *The Hunter's Moon*. She also writes non-fiction, including book reviews for the Tallahassee *Democrat,* and recently debuted her first comic book, *The Health Is Power League in Attack of ZomBacon*. An independent publisher, she worked with Lt. General Lawrence F. Snowden to publish his memoirs, *Snowden's Story*, and publishes the annual anthology of student narrative fiction contest winners for the Leon County Reading Council. She volunteers at the Eastside Branch Library and is an at-large member of the TWA Board of Directors. Visit her at turtlecovepress.com.

Katya Taylor – Haiku

Katya Sabaroff Taylor, M.Ed., is a writer (especially fond of haiku, but also short stories, essays, and other poetry forms) who has been offering creative writing (LifeStories and Haiku poetry) around Tallahassee since 1990. She is the author of *Journal Adventure Guidebook*, *My Haiku Life*, and *Prison Wisdom*, a compilation of writing done behind bars with inmates. She believes we all have a writer within us, and she enjoys the creative alchemy that happens when people write together. Please visit her website at creativeartsandhealing.com for more details.

Anna Yeatts – Flash Fiction

Anna Yeatts is the publisher of *Flash Fiction Online*, an online magazine for both literary and genre stories. Her own short fiction runs the gamut from horror and dark fantasy to more experimental, literary pieces. Anna's background is in biology and anatomy — always helpful when writing and reviewing body horror. She blogs occasionally for SF Signal's *Mindmeld*, the FlashBlog, and anywhere her opinion is allowed. Though Anna forever hopes to channel Shirley Jackson from the ether into her laptop as she searches for that perfect story, she recognizes this is a quest that will take a lifetime and beyond. Anna hides out in Pinehurst, North Carolina.

Joesphine Yu – Poetry

Josephine Yu earned an MFA from Georgia State University and a PhD from Florida State University. Her first manuscript, *Prayer Book of the Anxious*, won the Judge's Prize of the 15th Annual Elixir Press Poetry Awards and will be published in 2016. Her poems have appeared in such journals as *Ploughshares*, *The Southern Review*, *TriQuarterly*, and *Best New Poets 2008*. She won the Ploughshares 2013 Emerging Writers Contest and has been honored with Meridian's 2010 Editor's Prize, the New Letters 2010 Poetry Award, and the New Letters 2010–2011 Readers Award for Poetry.

2017 Reading Committee

A huge thank you is owed to our first readers. All are members in good standing of the Tallahassee Writers Association who contributed their time and attention in reviewing and pre-judging the submissions. These folks are the best!

Doug Alderson, Iain Baird, Alice Cappa, Katie Clark, Carla Detering, Lyla Ellzey, Linda Fisher, TJ Hapney, Al Hartman, Leigh Healey, Pamela Hutto, Joshua Jordan, Kevin Keating, Saundra Kelley, Jeff Lickson, Donna Meredith, Patrick Murphy, Oghenekome Onokpise, Jack Pitman, Lacey Rivers, Susan Tabaka-Kritzeck, Sydney Watson, Blue Whitaker, and Fotena Zirps.

2018 Seven Hills Literary Contest

Penumbra Poetry and Haiku Contest

2018 Call for Manuscripts

Seven Hills Literary Contest

Novel Except*: 3,000-word maximum, any genre; first chapter.

Young Adult Novel Excerpt*: 3,000-word maximum, any genre; first chapter.

Creative Non-Fiction: 3,000-word maximum (full manuscript), submissions in this genre could include (but are not limited to) memoir, food or travel writing, personal essays, new journalism, biography, non-fiction stories, and nature writing. The emphasis in creative non-fiction is on factually true yet elegant literary expression.

Short Story: 3,000-word maximum (full manuscript). An economy of setting and precise narration.

Children's Picture Book: 1,000-word maximum (full manuscript).

Flash Fiction: 500-word maximum (full manuscript).

*For Novel Excerpt and Young Adult Novel Excerpt, please add a 150-word (or less) plot synopsis at the beginning of the document. (Synopsis is not included in maximum word count.)

Penumbra Poetry and Haiku Contest

Poetry: Up to 50 lines, any style or subject; line length may be edited to fit final publication format.

Haiku: 3-line haiku should conform to 5-7-5 syllable count.

Prizes:

Literature (All Categories) and Poetry: 1st – $100; 2nd – $75; 3rd – $50

Haiku: 1st – $60; 2nd – $40; 3rd – $30

Seven Hills is a general circulation publication; no X-rated materials will be accepted. It is a blind publication; any evidence of the author's identity in the primary submission will disqualify the submission. Please provide a 150- to 200-word biography with your application: emphasis on who, what, why; your inspirations and aspirations; a little horn-tooting acceptable.

Deadline for Submissions: August 31, 2018

All submissions must go through the Submittable website:
https://sevenhillsreview.submittable.com/submit

Notes